4/11

£1. 50

Another Day, Another Match

The Diary of a County Cricketer's Season

BRIAN BRAIN

London
GEORGE ALLEN & UNWIN
Boston   Sydney

First published in 1981

GEORGE ALLEN & UNWIN LTD
40 Museum Street, London WC1A 1LU

© Brian Brain and Patrick Murphy, 1981

British Library Cataloguing in Publication Data

Brain, Brian
  Another day, another match.
  I. Title
  796.35'863'0924   GV921.G56

ISBN 0–04–796057–4

Set in 11 on 12 point Baskerville
by Nene Phototypesetters Ltd, Northampton
and printed in Great Britain
by Biddles Ltd, Guildford, Surrey

Contents

Illustrations

*All the photographs are the copyright of Ken Kelly, to whom grateful
acknowledgement is made*

Preface

The name of Brian Brain has never really set the cricketing world on fire, nor will it do so. I'm just a typical English county cricketer, one of about two hundred men who lead a strange existence throughout the apology for a summer. We get in our cars, drive a hundred miles or so, mooch around in dressing rooms, play cards when it rains, moan at the countless salads we have to eat, rub shoulders with the élite of the cricket world – and then drive away in our cars to another ground. Another day, another match. And never the glamour of a Test appearance to alter the atmosphere.

We play a lot of cricket and although it's even more enjoyable when you're successful, I still think it's a deeply satisfying life. After twenty-two years in the game (give or take a few years of exile) I'm now well paid for doing something I'd do for nothing. Some kids want to be engine drivers, soccer players or rock singers but I wanted to play cricket.

This diary is an attempt to portray the complex, itinerant world of a county cricketer as he tackles a demanding job in the fortieth year of his life. I trust it is written with very little hindsight; these are my thoughts at each stage of the season and I've resisted the temptation to alter opinions that have been invalidated by subsequent events.

I'm grateful to my genial team-mates at Gloucestershire County Cricket Club, to Tony Brown, an understanding secretary/manager, to our scorer, Bert Avery, for his statistical help, to all the friendly souls I meet in a typical season – and to Pat Murphy, for having the patience to guide me through this literary journal and help record my thoughts in coherent form.

BRIAN BRAIN
November 1980

Foreword

In cricket pavilions throughout England, the talk invariably gets round to those professionals unlucky enough to miss out on playing for their country. Such a man, beyond question, is Brian Maurice Brain.

Our paths first crossed in 1973 when he was playing for Worcestershire. I was not out overnight and reflected with some pleasure on the fact that I'd survived against the much-respected opening pair of Brian Brain and Vanburn Holder. My confidence didn't last long the following morning – it later transpired that their captain, Norman Gifford, had told Brian in his most trenchant manner that 'If that lanky so-and-so gets another ball pitched in his half of the wicket, that's the last bloody game you'll play for Worcestershire.' So I soon got a vicious lifter from Brian that I touched to the wicket-keeper. I spent the next couple of seasons ducking and weaving against Mr Brain, trying to work out how many half-volleys he'd bowled me. I only needed one hand. . . .

Fortunately my private torment was ended in 1976 when he joined Gloucestershire. The first half of that season only confirmed the adage that 'there's no smoke without fire' as we contemplated the reasons why such a fine bowler was sacked. We'd heard that he was moody and a bad influence in the dressing room and that he suffered a lot from pulled muscles. But soon he started delivering the goods and by the end of the season, Brian was a definite case of Gloucestershire's gain and Worcestershire's loss.

Since that year, our club's fortunes have fluctuated but Brian's contributions have been consistent. His bowling in all forms of cricket has been economical and penetrative (a rare achievement) and for a man who's bowled many overs in the last four decades, he's been remarkably injury-free.

Any young seam bowler would be well advised to study Brian's action. He gets very close to the stumps, thereby reducing the amount the ball needs to deviate to beat the bat, yet he's still resourceful enough to use the width of the crease to change the angle of delivery. His main delivery is the out-swinger to the right-hander (and how many seam bowlers can do that?), but he also has the priceless knack of bringing the ball into the batsman for a successful lbw appeal. One of his great qualities is that he rarely wastes the new ball, and neither does he try to bowl too quickly to the detriment of rhythm or accuracy. In case the reader thinks I'm biased, I can only confirm that Brian's prowess is held in high esteem by some of the world's leading batsmen, many of whom play in county cricket.

What of Brian Brain as a person? Well, physically he looks like an advert for a Third World charity poster and he's not exactly a devotee of unnecessary physical exertions. He belongs to the old school of players who enjoyed their night out on a Saturday and none of this chasing around on a Sunday for a game of forty-over rounders. He longs for his pint of lager and fag at 6.31 and I've never known how a man who takes six months off cricket manages to keep match-fit. Perhaps the Worcester air fortifies the over-forties.

As befits a man who's played such a long time, he speaks with great authority and knowledge on the way that cricket has changed. As such, he's a most constructive bridge between the old and the new in our game.

I've never known why Brian has so obviously lacked confidence in his own ability. I find it amazing that, at the end of a bad day, a bowler of his stature should suddenly decide that he has lost the ability to bowl. But that pessimistic side to his nature is the only real defect I've noticed in his character. We always change beside each other in dressing rooms up and down the land, and I've often been grateful to him for the time and effort he's put in to help me in the game. Brian Brain has a lot to offer cricket – and his readiness to offer encouragement, sympathy and advice to any player in the county championship speaks volumes for him and for the atmosphere of the game.

One of these seasons, I'll get the better of Brian by taking more wickets than him, but in a way I don't want that to happen for some time to come. If he even suspects that his wicket-taking abilities are on the wane, he won't hang around. And cricket – not just Gloucestershire cricket – needs Brian's commonsense, ability and respect for tradition for as long as possible.
DAVID GRAVENEY

March and April

Every year I experience the same feeling on my first day back at training: can I actually still bowl? Let's face it, even a superb athletic specimen like Brian Brain is getting no younger and there's bound to come the day when I just can't pitch it on a length. On 20 March I ran up and bowled my first delivery for six months – and it was on the spot. I keep waiting for the year when the ball will hit the side of the net but even though I'm fully aware that my number is bound to be up in first-class cricket fairly soon, I'll keep going as long as I'm useful to the side and don't feel a passenger. Clearly the club feel that that time is some distance away because they've appointed me senior professional, as right-hand man to the captain, Mike Procter. That's a great honour for me, because I've had my disciplinary ups and downs in the game – particularly with my former county, Worcestershire – and although I wasn't totally innocent, I honestly feel I've pulled my weight since coming to Gloucestershire in 1976. Mike Procter knows how to treat me, he gives me a kick up the backside on occasions, and I have a great respect for the man's playing ability and what he has done for the county.

I don't spend the six months between the English seasons flitting from ground to ground throughout the world. I make do with weighty matters like finding a job, paying the bills and perfecting my darts skills. For the first fortnight after the season ends, I'm glad of the break but I soon get the yen for the game. So much so that I spend the winter preparing myself really professionally – I train on twenty fags and a couple of pints of lager a day and a prolonged diet of cricket talk. It never fails to pep me up for the fray. The other lads may have better suntans than me when we re-assemble at nets in the spring but I'm the one who's only slightly overweight compared with September. Don't ask me how I do it, but I'm delighted to say

1

that my 11 stone 9 lbs sits easily enough on my 6 feet 2 ins frame. So, after my rigorous winter of self-denial, I'm raring to go.

In fact everybody looked very fit on that first day back; the overseas players – Procter and the two Pakistanis, Sadiq and Zaheer – were still abroad but it was good to feel the comradeship of what is a very friendly side and club. It was a pleasant change not to see the ground covered in water and to be able to get out into the middle in the first week. Indoor nets are all very well but they're not much use for a pace bowler. He needs space to iron out his run-up and develop rhythm; the short run-ups in the indoor nets put too much strain on the bowler's body early on, when he's feeling a little rusty.

In the absence of Procter, I've been in charge of playing matters while working with our secretary/manager, Tony Brown, and I have done a fair amount of TV, radio and newspaper interviews at the start of the season. I am asked the same question by everyone – is this going to be Gloucestershire's year? I've played long enough to know what makes a title-winning side and at this stage, I feel we haven't got the necessary bowling balance. Our two left-arm spinners, John Childs and David Graveney, are fine bowlers but we need a world-class spinner. Most wickets at Bristol are slow ones and our spinners do bowl a lot of overs. We need a Gifford, an Emburey or an Underwood, someone who will take 8 for 25 rather than 5 for 60. Childs finds bowling a cricket ball much easier than Graveney, who's a big lad and rather cumbersome, but although David lacks his partner's natural gifts, he worked terribly hard in the nets during the winter and won't fail for lack of effort. I really admire David. His father, Ken, is a former Gloucestershire captain and the club's present chairman while Tom, his uncle, was a great batsman, yet David has gone his own way in this club and his selection has been purely on his own merits. Both Childs and Graveney are lovely lads who genuinely like each other and enjoy bowling together but they must learn to bowl six good balls an over: it's no use getting the batsman to block four good deliveries in a row only for him to smash the last two in the over for eight runs. In English cricket, that kind of stuff is meat and drink to the Rices, Lambs, Bothams and Davisons.

We've also got a problem in the pace bowling department;

neither Procter nor myself is exactly in the first flush of youth and we badly need a good support seamer. We've signed Alan Wilkins from Glamorgan and the Cambridge Blue, David Surridge, to fill that gap. We need someone who can tie up one end with sensible line and length bowling, while Procter and I have a rest – even more vital if there's nothing in the wicket for the spinners. Wilkins has a fair amount of experience in county cricket but at the moment I'm more impressed with Surridge. He's learned his trade at Fenner's, a batsman's paradise where you've simply got to bowl line and length, and one of his great assets is that he can bowl straight. That's a great plus in the limited-over stuff – towards the end of the innings when the slog is on, if you keep bowling straight you'll pick up wickets because the batsmen are bound to miss a few. Surridge hits the seam four times an over, he can swing it and I think he's a very good acquisition.

I'll be looking to some of our younger players for improvement. My driving partner on all those interminable journeys up the motorways is David Partridge; despite his habit of dropping off to sleep as soon as he gets in my car at the start of a 200-mile journey, he's a good lad with a lot of ability. He made some good-looking runs last year but although he bowled his medium pace well on occasions, he seemed to tire – surprising really, considering what a splendid physique he has. It was his first full season of championship cricket and that takes a lot out of anybody so it'll be interesting to see how he develops this season. And if he can stay awake a little longer in the car, I'll be more than grateful.

We'll all be expecting a lot from Phil Bainbridge. When he first came to prominence in the 1978 season, I told anyone polite enough to listen that he'd bat for England within the next five years. That's the kiss of death, I suppose, and when he went off to teachers' training college his batting declined. He played on too many inferior wickets and got away with playing across the line. So when he came back into county cricket, it was a nightmare – wise old birds would make mental notes and Phil wouldn't last very long. But in his first month of training, he has looked much sounder. He's worked hard in the winter nets and I think he's back to the good habits of 1978. And he's still only 22. . . .

I'm hoping our youngsters will put the pressure on our three world-class overseas players, simply by performing well. I know that sometimes our three blokes have felt that they lacked support from the rest of our side and that may have been so. But if Andy Stovold gets 1,500 runs this season, there'll be a lot of pressure on Zaheer to top that with 2,000 and for Sadiq to make 1,800. If I pick up eighty championship wickets, then Procter will feel he has to get 100; that's the way their minds work, and that's fair enough. They have their professional pride and they've all done this county proud – but by putting extra pressure on them by our own performances, we should be able to get that little bit extra from Sadiq, Zaheer and Procter and then the side will benefit accordingly. The English-born players must guard against getting complacent, thinking, 'Oh, Sadiq will go out and smash a hundred and Procter's good for a quick 70' because the day is not far off when we'll have to do with just one overseas player in the side. The Test and County Cricket Board is cutting down on the amount of overseas players per team to encourage the development of home-grown talent, so we must start thinking now about replacements in the next couple of years. And who knows? A bit of local pride may make us more successful in the eighties.

There's extra pressure this season on all three overseas players. 'Proc' can't keep playing cricket round the year. He's done remarkably well to keep going for so long and some of his performances last summer with bat and ball were superb. But I know he wasn't fully fit throughout the South African season and we're all wondering just how long he will want to keep going as strike bowler/major batsman/occasional off-spinner/captain. My own feeling is that if Gloucestershire don't get the scent of success this season, then he will stay on for a few more seasons because he's not the type to quit and leave a sinking ship to someone else. He hates losing, but he puts on a brave face and can take the flak that always comes a losing captain's way. Last season he was worried about the effect of the break-up of World Series Cricket on his career and business life and also about his son's education, but son Gregg will be staying in South Africa all year now and Mike seems happy with the arrangement.

I don't think any of us really blamed Procter and Zaheer for signing for Packer in 1977. For a few days we knew that something was going on, but Proc and 'Zed' were sworn to secrecy

4

and not even our chairman, Ken Graveney, was in on it. When it all came out, no one really knew what to say in our dressing room; my attitude was that if you could earn nearly £20,000 a year for playing cricket, good luck. No one in his right mind could turn it down and I wouldn't condemn anyone for signing for Packer, as long as he realised that he couldn't play Test cricket for his country at the same time. Our biggest concern was whether they were going to be banned from county cricket. As far as I'm concerned, a county cricketer is a free agent in the English winter and the club can't stop him playing elsewhere, provided it doesn't affect his performances next season. When I first started in the game, I was paid two-thirds of my salary in the summer and the rest in the winter, so I had to do what I was told by Worcestershire all the year round. But now, if Gloucestershire want me to turn up at a function for them in December, I'm perfectly entitled to refuse, because I'm not employed by them at that time. On that basis, it seemed wrong to try to ban the Packer players from county cricket, because WSC wasn't interfering with it.

Both Procter and Zaheer say that WSC also benefited non-Packer players, and I agree. It helped to bring the minimum wage structure forward after several years' discussion and more counties are now aware of the importance of looking after the players financially. In my first season with Gloucestershire in 1976, my contract was £2,100 plus bonuses, yet this season its £4,850 plus bonuses. Players are now getting a reasonable standard of living from the game, and not before time.

I think Packer cricket has altered the way some of his players now bat. Procter doesn't get into line as much as he used to do and both Zaheer and Gordon Greenidge are more two-eyed in their stance. That's not surprising, considering they had to face the fastest bowlers in the world, coming at you off a conveyor belt – Procter was fifth bowler on many occasions in the World Side! Playing cricket continuously for nearly three months against blokes who bounce it halfway down the wicket must affect your technique. Perhaps that's why Zaheer was dropped by Pakistan this winter; he's got a great Test record and something must have gone radically wrong with a technique that's got him so many runs around the world. But we feel that his dropping may rebound in our favour – he hates sitting in the pavilion after being dismissed and I think he'll do

5

his best to stay out there in the middle and prove the Pakistan selectors were wrong. Zed's got an immense amount of professional pride and he loves getting big scores, both for his country and for Gloucestershire. He told me last season that he missed not seeing his Packer runs included in the first-class records and he's delighted to be able to get the chance to set more records. He wants to do things that'll take a great deal of surpassing – he'd love to get 3,000 runs in an English season for a start – and he'll have a lot to prove this summer.

So will Zed's fellow-countryman, Sadiq; he's eligible for a benefit in 1982 and he won't want to throw that chance away so he'll be looking for consistency for the next couple of years. Sadiq has a strong sense of professional pride. Early last season, when he was dropped because he was playing badly, other Test players would have sulked and blamed it on everything except themselves but he worked hard in the nets, won his way back into the side and ended up with eight championship centuries.

Basically we've got a young side, apart from that venerable opening pair of M. J. Procter and B. M. Brain. I think we're just a little too young to win a trophy; a successful team needs about five experienced young cricketers in the 28/30-year-old bracket, plus a couple of old hands. In two years' time I think we'll be a really good outfit, but at least it's the best squad of players I've yet played with at Bristol, and if we can score our runs quickly enough to give us time to bowl the opposition out, we could surprise a few people. But there are no easy games any more; we play the Minor Counties next month in the Benson and Hedges Cup and I don't think that'll be easy on the Chippenham ground. It's a small ground, and you never know what that wicket will do. I can't forget that last year they could have got 250 against us in the tie at Bristol, but their best batsman (Richard Lewis, the former Hampshire opener) went to pieces when he'd done the difficult bit and worn us down. So we won't be taking any match for granted – we owe that to our supporters as well as to ourselves.

At this time of the year, the players talk about the season's prospects with the same enthusiasm as any press or public bar pundit and, like many others, I can't see past Essex and Kent. Experience, strength in depth and talent count for so much. I'm not so sure about Somerset, though, as they'll miss a few

The pre-season slog. Notice the time on the pavilion clock as I set off to jog round the Bristol ground (above). Then it's into the gym for a session on the weights, with sadistic Andy Stovold as taskmaster (below).

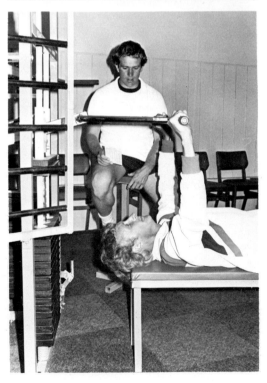

The opening championship game at Worcester and Mike Procter, fresh from the sunshine of Durban, tries to adapt to the cold. Almost as many players as spectators attended the first day's play.

An everyday story of Gloucester-shire folk when rain stops play. While Alastair Hignell and Alan Wilkins pore over *The Times* crossword and Sadiq catches up with the world's news (below), Messrs Brain and Graveney seek solace in rather less intellectual pursuits – a cup of tea and a fag (left).

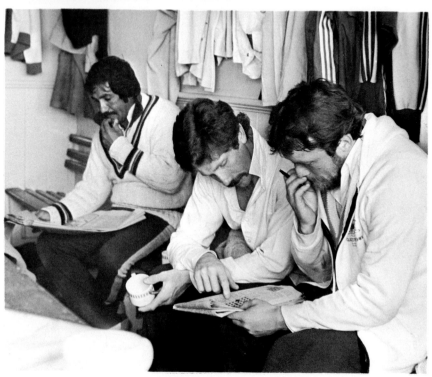

I'm not used to blowing my own trumpet but I've always maintained that I have a good bowling action and I'm glad to say Ken Kelly's pictures bear me out.

players through Test calls. But they do have some players who rarely grab the headlines, yet are respected by the county pros – men like Derek Taylor, Peter Denning and Phil Slocombe – not to mention a young man who makes the most of his abilities, Vic Marks. He's a gritty, unselfish batsman who sells his wicket dearly and as an off-spinner, he's not afraid to give it some air and vary his pace. A player to watch.

Not surprisingly, the West Indies are grabbing a lot of headlines this month. They're being built up as superstars with their fast bowlers supposedly the meanest warriors since Attila the Hun and his merry men. Well, I hope they behave themselves rather better than on the tour of New Zealand when they made the umpires' lives a misery. Things went on out in Australia that had no place on the cricket field. There were the antics of the West Indians, Ian Chappell's swearing and histrionics and the petulance of Dennis Lillee, but the English lads weren't exactly blameless either, from what I could see on the box. I don't see why the umpires should be constantly hassled and I'm sure ours won't stand for any nonsense this summer. Quite right too.

At the moment, there's never been a better chance of getting into the England side in my experience. Almost every position is up for grabs after the disastrous tour of Aussie. I'm not surprised at our batsmen's failings out there; any experienced bowler in county cricket will tell you that England lacks solid, sensible batsmen who can build an innings. Men like Barrington, Graveney, Cowdrey and May wouldn't have thrown their wickets away like our lot last winter. They're getting paid exceedingly well for not playing professionally. David Gower, in particular, makes my blood boil. I can name thirty other English players who wouldn't have sold their wickets as cheaply as Gower in the winter. He should be left in county cricket for a season to learn his trade. It would break my heart to miss out on all that money by dropping out of the England scene, so perhaps Gower will eventually realise cricket's not always about champagne, it's a bread-and-butter game.

If Bob Woolmer had gone to Australia as Boycott's partner, things would have been different, I'm sure, but Packer politics perhaps ruled that out. As it is, I feel Woolmer must be recalled this summer. Let's face it, we will lose the series, so why not build for the future? Two months away from the First Test, I can name only six certainties: Boycott, Woolmer, Gooch, Botham, Underwood and Dilley. I hope Mike Hendrick gets fit in time as he's the best medium-pacer around, in my opinion. How many half-volleys do you see him bowl? He's tight and disciplined, he gets wickets for other bowlers by his nagging accuracy and he's a brilliant slip fielder. But apart from these few players, the cupboard looks pretty bare. It's time to give chances to batsmen like Cook of Northants, Parker of Sussex and Richard Lumb of Yorkshire, batsmen who won't play airy-fairy shots when a bowler ties them down. And batsmen with the guts to withstand a pace barrage that will be unrelenting.

Who will captain England? Well, the press will do their best to give it to Botham, although it remains to be seen whether he grows into the job. At least he's worth his place in the side, an argument that rules out men like Roger Knight of Surrey and Somerset's Brian Rose, batsmen who aren't all that superior to Mike Brearley in my opinion. Botham has great natural ability – although I always fancy bowling at him because he plays loosely – and he would lead from the front in the Tony Greig style. But I think he might attack at the wrong times. There are times when you simply have to defend – something that Greig painfully discovered in the 1976 series against the West Indians – and that would be totally against Botham's rather headstrong nature. And I'd be happier if Botham was also captain of Somerset; I don't think occasional leadership is the best training for captaining England.

I'd like to see Keith Fletcher get the job. He's the best tactician in England; he never gets flustered and is also a fine player. Since he started wearing the helmet, he's perfectly sound against the fast bowlers and the whisper that he's not happy against the quicks now belongs to history. It's a long time since Lillee and Thomson in 1974–75 on lightning-fast Australian wickets where nobody really looked the part, and no one has ever doubted Fletcher's ability as a batsman. I doubt if he'll get the nod, though, because Fleet Street wants Botham. He would be good box-office, his flamboyance would make good headline material. Any pro cricketer will tell you that the press can help pick the England team, that the selectors may take notice of respected writers like Michael Melford and John Woodcock.

The inadequacies of the England set-up were a regular topic

8

of discussion in our dressing room but the main cricketing considerations at Bristol were to get a good sound start to build up our confidence. Things went well. The dry weather allowed us plenty of time for match practice, we had the better of two practice games against Worcestershire and Glamorgan and so we came to the opening first-class match at Oxford. The designation 'first-class' is something M. J. Procter would take issue with; no offence to either Oxford or Cambridge but Proc doesn't recognise them as first-class matches, whatever the TCCB might say. He calls for the averages at the end of each month to assess everyone's progress and he refuses to have the Oxford and Cambridge figures included. Players *do* take notice of averages, no matter what they say. Over a season they're a relevant guide but I do wish a bowler's striking rate was better valued, rather than his ability to keep the score down. A captain would rather his bowler took 6 for 70 in ten overs than 2 for 30 in twenty-five overs of a championship match because three-day cricket is more to do with bowling sides out than just containing them. I think the first-class bowling averages should be assessed on striking rate, rather than wickets per runs.

Proc came to watch us at Oxford and he saw me proudly lead out the side as captain for the first time in a career stretching back to 1959. My fourth decade in first-class cricket began in happy circumstances and the overall atmosphere was very pleasant. Basically we were there for practice, so I didn't enforce the follow-on when we bowled them out for next to nothing. Chris Broad, our young left-hand opener, got a hundred before lunch and although he was given rather a lot of half-volleys, he used his long reach well and whacked 'em. I suggested he went in first because he's not the greatest player of spin bowling; Andy Stovold, our regular opener with Sadiq, is happy to drop down and that will strengthen our middle order.

In the second innings, I reversed our batting order and put David Graveney in ahead of David Partridge. I did that just to gee them up because they both tend to have a little go at each other, each believing he should bat ahead of the other. I thought 'Grav's' longer reach would be better against the new ball and so it proved. He shows the maker's name to the bowler when he pushes forward and his long reach does upset some of them. At one stage he was playing so well that I had to walk round the ground, motioning to him to cool it. The way he was batting we looked like having a lead of 600.

We had two very pleasant social evenings during the Oxford match. On the first night, both sides had dinner together at Vincent's, a University sporting club. To celebrate my fourth decade in the game I bought a few bottles of bubbly and we organised the seating arrangements so that both sides could mix. We tried to help the Oxford lads with some constructive criticism and they were very good listeners. They'll find it hard this season and Cambridge are a far better side, but at least they're willing to learn. Oxford do have a couple of good bowlers – the young off-spinner Sutcliffe looks useful and the captain, Jon Ross, is a fine new-ball bowler. Alan Gibson of *The Times* doesn't think so; in one of his reports of the match, he cast doubts on Jon's abilities. That annoyed me because Mr Gibson's article consisted of just a few lines about the actual game and the rest of it was an 'atmosphere' piece. If he'd written about one of my players in the same dismissive way, I would have had a few words with Mr Gibson.

Alastair Hignell provided us with some merriment when the game was over. I gave him a bowl right at the death to see if we could get a drink out of him. At Gloucestershire we have a system whereby you have to buy a round of drinks whenever you notch a career best for the county, whether in bowling or batting. What you did for other sides is irrelevant, so the best thing to do is to get a hundred or take six wickets right at the start because every time you improve on your performances for Gloucestershire, the old hand must go in the pocket. My first year with them in 1976 cost me £78 in drinks, including a £14 round in a doubles bar in Southampton! Anyway, Alastair was brought on with his leg-breaks and he bowled one very tidy over, he got his first wicket for the county and we delightedly toasted his health afterwards!

All in all, it was an enjoyable opening to the first-class season. And there was one little perk enjoyed by the senior professional and stand-in captain – a room to myself. Not a Partridge snore to be heard.

So to our first championship match. It's at Worcester, my home, and the place where I learned my cricket. I always like playing against the county that sacked me in 1975 because they thought I was too old – it's nothing personal, in fact I have a very good relationship now with everyone at New Road, but it's a matter of professional pride that I pull out that little bit extra against my old team. I had some happy times there, sharing in three county championship wins, winning a John Player League medal and appearing in two limited-over finals at Lord's, but there's no doubt in my mind that going to Bristol was the best thing I ever did. We all get into a professional rut at some stage in our careers and Mike Procter gave me the sort of inspiration I needed. I'd see him charging in off his long run with his wonky knees and think, 'God, if he can keep going, well, so can I.'

I love Worcester. It's peaceful, friendly and near to the kind of motorway system any professional cricketer needs. My club is very understanding about my desire to remain living there. My wife, Eve, is a teacher and she and my three daughters (18-year-old Sarah and 15-year-old twins Helen and Susan) are happy in the area where they were all brought up. So I travel 130 miles a day when playing at Bristol and 12,000 miles in all per season, but that's my choice and I can't complain about it.

We all complained about the weather at Worcester, though. Not a brass monkey was to be seen, and when Sadiq put on his long johns we all sympathised – even more so when he was hit a stinging blow on the thigh by Worcestershire's new West Indian fast bowler, Hartley Alleyne. This bloke looked very sharp indeed and he won a psychological battle with Sadiq. Now Sadiq's a shrewd little fellow and whenever a new black fast bowler is playing for the opposition, he always makes a point of going into their dressing room, shaking hands, introducing himself and wishing the newcomer lots of luck in English cricket. Sadiq figures that this will decrease his chances of getting his head knocked off with a bouncer. Anyway, Hartley Alleyne scuppered Sadiq because he went up to him and Zaheer and said, 'You won't remember me, but I bowled against you both in the nets before a Test Match back home in Barbados.' That must be a great feeling for the lad to play against them now – and he had Sadiq caught and Zaheer dropped, so he won this particular contest. He bowled 23 overs in the day and he was still quick in the final one. He never took his long-sleeved sweater off and when the wickets get harder, I think he'll be quite a proposition. He certainly looks wild enough – when a catch was dropped off his bowling, he jumped

11

up and down and looked very West Indian.

Zaheer played a patchy innings. He tells me that he's reverted to wearing glasses this season because the dust kept getting behind his contact lenses during the winter and that's why he batted poorly. In this cold weather Zed still looks a little lost, but I'm convinced the brilliance and the hunger for runs is still there, and I noticed he still hasn't lost the ability to get onto his toes and play a fast ball over the top of the bounce through the gully area. Very few batsmen in the world can play over a sharply rising ball as safely as Zed.

Proc was caught and bowled by Norman Gifford, playing a soft-hearted shot. Proc should never just block it, he looks so much better going for his shots. Even if he mishits, his strength often takes the ball beyond the fielder and over the boundary. When he came back into the dressing room I said, 'That didn't sting Norman's hands very much, did it?' and Proc said, 'Well, how do you think I should play?' There's only one answer to that – like he did towards the end of last season when he set his sights on the fastest hundred of the summer and proceeded to slaughter the bowlers until he'd reached the target. Proc gets out when he tries to play thoughtfully. Mind you, I'd hate to be the next man in because I'm never at ease when he's at the crease. With Zaheer, I'm totally relaxed because I never think he's going to get out when he's batting well, but Proc is vulnerable, even though compulsive watching. I feel sorry for Alastair Hignell this season; he has to follow Proc if he's played magnificently, while at the same time he'll be on the edge of his seat expecting to be in any minute now, while Proc flirts with danger.

I picked up my first championship wicket of the season when I had Alan Ormrod caught down the leg-side by our keeper, Andy Brassington. It's ironic, really – my first county cricket wicket last season was also at Worcester, although there was a bit of a time difference. Even though I bowled well, and the weather robbed us of a lot of cricket, I didn't get that wicket till 11 June. I got to the stage where I thought, 'To hell with this. I've got no wickets bowling decent deliveries, I'm going to try to get them with rubbish ones,' and then I worried about getting back into my groove. It was a worrying time which I hope I can steer clear of this season, or else the knockers will start whispering about the imminence of my fortieth birthday.

12

As if I need reminding! My memory is jogged almost every day in our dressing room.

The best batting of the Worcester match came from Glenn Turner. He got a double hundred and made it all look so easy. After thirty overs he'd scored only 38 but then he slipped up a couple of gears and mastered the length of the ball. He hit a lot of sixes, all of them in the mid-wicket area. Two of them were off my bowling, although I bowled fairly well at him: right up in the blockhole, trying to get him to swing across the line. I dropped just a couple short and he pulled me over the short boundary. Turner paces an innings so well and his placement of shot is so certain. Early on, he edged me but it didn't carry to gully. Then he padded me away and everyone went up for an appeal. I was sure it was out, Glenn didn't look at the umpire (a sure sign it was close) but Barry Meyer gave him the benefit of the doubt. At the end of the over I said to Barry, 'That must have been close,' and he said, 'Yes, but you bowled it too near to the stumps. If you'd delivered the ball a little wider of the crease, the angle would have favoured the break-back and he would have been out.' I thought that was a terrific piece of umpiring; there was no need for one of the best in the country to justify anything to me and that incident only deepened my respect for the English first-class umpire.

In the end, the game fizzled out. Norman Gifford delayed his declaration and it all got pretty meaningless. The same thing happened a couple of years ago when we decided to bat out on a flat wicket that favoured the batsmen and the crowd at Worcester gave us some almighty stick. Cricketers have long memories, but so do the spectators.

From what I could judge in this game, Worcestershire will be hard-pressed to match their fine achievement of finishing second in the championship last season. Younis, who did so well for them in 1979, looks a stone overweight and I don't think he will be so consistent this time round. He doesn't seem to know how to play the forward defensive shot, he's an 'all or nothing' player. They don't have any adequate cover for their wicket-keeper, David Humphries, and I just don't know what they'll do if he breaks a finger. Their bowling isn't all that strong, either – Gifford's still a fine bowler, Inchmore an under-rated seamer and Alleyne should do well – but that's not the basis of a trophy-winning side. In fact their assets and

13

defects are roughly similar to ours at Gloucestershire.

There was plenty of banter among the lads during the evenings at Worcester. One night, most of them came down to my local to see the darts skills of the demon Brain; unfortunately the talents I'd earbashed them about seemed to wither in front of their sceptical eyes and I played like an idiot. I won back some points the following night, though, at a cricket quiz in West Bromwich. We played Worcestershire and our side (Alastair Hignell, David Graveney, Andy Stovold, David Surridge and myself) easily triumphed over Dipak Patel, David Humphries, Barry Jones, Martin Weston and their guest, Barry Meyer. Well what do you expect with Cambridge graduates like Hignell and Surridge in the team? I was only selected for the pre-1940 questions but I surprised a few with the right answer to the question: 'Name the uncapped player who is now captain of his county side?' – Nick Pocock, of Hampshire, as if you didn't know. Then there was a real teaser: we had to name eighteen players who'd made more than sixty appearances for England. We got sixteen of them and I was very surprised that Peter May was one of them. It was a very enjoyable evening, but our lads are particularly good at things like that. We had to leave the ground as soon as play ended to drive thirty-five miles to the venue and nobody moaned about missing the Arsenal–Liverpool FA Cup semi-final on the box. It's good public relations, something many pro cricketers forget about as they rush around from fixture to fixture. Gloucestershire may not be the most successful county side but I'd defend us against any team on matters of sociability, friendliness and good temper.

One final word on Worcester, concerning the evil, cold weather as much as the sufferer, Hartley Alleyne. Most of us who are used to such conditions were in a bad enough way during the match but God knows how poor Hartley must have felt. After all, he'd been whisked from the sunshine of Barbados only a couple of weeks earlier. Anyway, David Humphries told me how Hartley had learned to cope with the cold; one day 'Humpty' opened the airing cupboard to fetch out a clean, warm towel, only to find himself staring through the dark at two large white eyes! There was Hartley, sitting in the gloom of the airing cupboard – but at least he was warm! That's a story that'll do the rounds of the county circuit this season. . . .

14

May

The first match of the month showed how much we've got to do before we can claim to be a good all-round side. Northants needed the highest total of the championship game – over 300 – but they strolled it by eight wickets. Procter's declaration was a fair one and an unselfish one, considering that he was well in line for the fastest hundred of the season. But Zaheer dropped young Williams as soon as he came in and he and Allan Lamb then gave us an object lesson in chasing a big total. I hope our lads took notice of the calm, professional way Northants batted because we've never been a good 'chasing' side; we often get to 60 for 2 off twelve overs, then 125 for 7 and 145 all out. We don't seem to be able to get a solid platform of about two runs an over for the first twenty overs, then build on it.

Northants must have the five best batsmen in a row in the county championship; no other side can compare with them for a contrasting blend of strokeplay and solid professionalism. Geoff Cook is a really fine, old-fashioned opener in the sense that he doesn't give his wicket away, plays for the side and builds a platform for the more brilliant later batsmen to exploit. Cook's opening partner, Wayne Larkins, gets more headlines but I know who I'd rather bowl at. Larkins is a fine, free strokeplayer and he's bound to play a few superb innings every season which will dazzle the press box. But Cook knows his limitations and is very hard to get out. Proc has played Currie Cup cricket against him for the past two seasons and I know he rates him highly.

The lad who impressed me most in the Northants batting line-up was Richard Williams. When he first came into the game, he did what a lot of young players do – he blocked and blocked. But now, after a couple of seasons, he gives it a whack if it's anywhere near him. I know a lot of critics say he won't get very far because he's so small but he didn't seem in any trouble

15

against Proc or myself. I suppose someone like Joel Garner will trouble him with his steep bounce, but then players a foot taller than Williams have the same problem. He's not the worst off-spinner, either, and with a slightly round-arm action he's difficult to slog because he doesn't get much bounce. The lad's got all-round ability and it won't be long before people start trying to talk him into the England team, but to be honest, I can't see him being anything more than a very good and valuable county player. I wonder if that little forecast will make me look a fool in a few years' time.

I admire Peter Willey. He's a professional's cricketer. Willey's had the kind of knee trouble that would have finished off many other players but he fought back, worked out his batting technique and adjusted to bowling off-spinners. When he first came into the game, I thought he'd be a very fine player, but his injuries held him back. I'm not sure where he can fit in under the present regime with the England side. I've no idea where they could bat him; surely not as low as number 7? Or as an opener? I hope he does well, he's a nice guy and in the right frame of mind he can really take an attack apart – as I found out to my cost on the last day of our game.

Then there's Allan Lamb. I think this bloke could be the batsman of the 'eighties. He's such a dominant player. When he came in to bat in the second innings, he played a couple of brilliant shots almost at once and I thought, 'Christ, we've got to get this bloke out now or he'll murder us.' He did, and his century won the match. There's just no safe length to bowl at Lamb; he doesn't need a half-volley to play through the covers. He presents the full face of the bat to the bowler and hits through the line – in other words he doesn't have to wait till the ball is on him before selecting his stroke, he seems to know instinctively a split second early that the ball is going down a particular line. I was delighted when I got him out in the first innings. Proc told me that Lamb didn't play the hook but he would pull if the ball was in the right place. I bowled him a bouncer and he wafted at it and missed so I thought, 'Right, I'll try him with a quicker one next over.' It was a yard quicker and he was caught behind. He made me suffer for that in the second innings, though.

I've yet to see a bad South African cricketer over here. It must be a combination of learning the game on good wickets, strength of character, competitive instinct and natural ability. But this bloke Lamb looks as if he could be the best of the lot. There's a lot of talk flying around that he could play for England in four years time because his parents are English and he hasn't played for the country of his birth. As far as I'm concerned, if he's eligible then, like Tony Greig, he should be considered for England selection, but I'd love to see us in a position to be able to say, 'We don't need you.' It would be great to find about six young Englishmen with the batting class of Allan Lamb. Somehow I can't see that happening.

Quite apart from our defeat, another thing upset me in the Northants match: Alastair Hignell had his nose broken when he was fielding at short leg and it was my fault. I'd bowled twenty-six overs and was knackered. I sent down a leg-side half-volley to a tailender, Tim Lamb. Now a good player would have hit such a ball through mid-on for a boundary, but Tim didn't pick his bat up at all and just whipped the ball away. The ball hit Alastair with an awful crack, he went down on all fours and simply said, 'I'll be all right. Don't worry.' He's been hit at short leg a few times – he wears a box and occasionally shinpads, but never a helmet because he says it restricts his vision. I fancy he'll wear one in the future. He's always had confidence that our bowlers won't bowl any loose stuff on the leg stump and I felt I'd let him down. For a couple of overs after the injury I didn't want to bowl and I certainly didn't like to ask anyone else to stand at short leg for me. David Graveney stood there – with a helmet. I went to see 'Higgie' in hospital that night after his operation and said, 'What can I say?' Back came the reply. 'Nothing. It was my fault because I chose not to wear the helmet.' The surgeons did a great job on his hooter, and in fact we all agree that he looks better than ever after the operation.

One silver lining to the cloud of the Northants game: we all did well on the horses. My old Worcestershire team-mate, Jim Yardley, gave us a couple of tips, our team put £2 each into the kitty and they sailed in at 9–1 and 11–4 so we were about £600 richer. A great lad is Jim Yardley, quite apart from his expertise with the nags. He'll get 600 runs a season in the county championship, take some blinding catches at slip and never moan about a thing. He's got his own style of batting which involves exploring the third man territory. A lot of captains think he's edging the ball when he plays this shot, but in fact he's placing it. I've seen Brian Close put four gullies and two men at third man for Jim Yardley – yet he still got the ball through them! Very rarely does he hit the ball straight, you can bowl at him without a mid-off or mid-on.

Another under-rated man in that Northants side is their seamer, Jim Griffiths. He bowled very well against us in the Sunday League game, which we lost comfortably. He's got a high arm action, hits the deck and has the ability to bowl a very good delivery. Yet few people ever talk about Jim Griffiths outside the dressing rooms – he just gets on with the game.

I always like playing against Northants. I've known their skipper, Jim Watts, since the 'fifties and there's a nice atmosphere in his side. I always felt sorry for them playing at that bleak Northampton ground but the facilities have greatly improved there, I understand. Perhaps I was spoiled, learning my trade at Worcester, but I could never understand how anyone would want to play regularly at Northampton. I'm pleased for a great bunch of lads that things are looking up there.

One other thing that stood out in that Northants match – the cold. It was bloody freezing. The opposition had hot beef tea brought out to them when they were fielding but we couldn't afford that luxury because of our slow over-rate. We are supposed to bowl nineteen overs an hour but, with Procter and Brain bowling long spells, that is rather tricky. If we fail to get that target, the players are fined £500 and the club the same amount for each half of the season. We often find ourselves in the position of having to bowl twenty-eight overs an hour to catch up with the over-rate, and by the end of the Northants game we were already thirty overs adrift. That's why we often play two spinners when the wicket isn't turning: if the batsmen think Childs and Graveney are bowling long spells because it's a spinners' wicket, well that's fine, but sometimes it's for no other reason than to improve our over-rate. There's nothing much we can do about that, because Proc needs a long run-up to generate pace and I need to bowl off nineteen strides to get rhythm.

The cold had a lot to do with my picking up a groin injury. I felt it stiffen up after the Northants game and it got worse as I drove home. I thought I had no chance of playing the next day against Glamorgan but Les Bardsley, our physiotherapist, rubbed it loose and said, 'Go out and try it – it won't get any worse.' I felt better and Proc wanted me to play, so I did and picked up six wickets in the first innings. But it went in the second innings. It felt as if a red-hot needle had been stuck in my groin. I'd only had groin trouble once before – in 1976, when I missed ten weeks in my first season with Gloucestershire. That one was a lot worse because it was in the left groin, which affects my delivery stride. This one was in the right groin, so I was hopeful I'd soon be fit for the important fortnight ahead with the Benson and Hedges matches looming. Since my 1976 groin injury, I'd always done stretching exercises before coming on to bowl, so I could only assume this injury was due to the extreme cold.

The championship defeat by Glamorgan was bad enough (their first victory in the championship for two years, incidentally) but then they beat us by one run in the Benson and Hedges Cup the following day. We were unlucky in the three-day game, with Procter unable to bowl because of a shoulder injury, my groin injury flaring up again and Alan Wilkins ruled out with an allergy. I got 15 in each innings which just shows how fallible our batting was becoming. At this rate I'll be batting number 5 with my trusty helmet and visor by my side – just my luck for it to be against the West Indies! Glamorgan's new captain, Malcolm Nash, picked up eleven wickets in the match and although he swung the ball a lot, at his pace he shouldn't be rolling over class batsmen. He forked out a few quid for a couple of bottles of champagne once Javed Miandad's hundred had won the game.

The B & H game was a classic example of our ability to snatch defeat from the jaws of victory. We needed to win this one to have any chance of qualifying because we knew the games against Essex and Sussex would be tough. Procter couldn't bowl again. He suffers from scar tissue just above the collar bone, which he picked up playing rugby a few years back. Normally he bowls through it at the start of the season but it's been so cold that he hasn't been able to bowl all that much. He'll just have to wait till it gets warmer – will that ever happen? I was also unfit, but our young replacement bowlers, Wilkins, Surridge, Bainbridge and Broad, did very well to contain Glamorgan. We put them in because we felt we were better chasing a target rather than defending it with an inexperienced

19

bowling side. We needed 220-odd to win and we were walking it most of the way. But Procter, Zaheer and Andy Stovold all got out when well set. The crucial dismissal was Zed's. He hit the first ball of Nash's second spell just short of a six, but straight into the fielder's hands on the boundary. For a batsman of Zed's calibre to get in, establish himself and then throw it away was inexcusable. That's just giving your wicket away and you deserve to lose if you play like that. I hope the weather soon bucks up, so that Zed can get back to scoring big hundreds again.

In the last over we needed ten to win, and we only got eight of them. Before the last ball, David Graveney went down the wicket and told Alan Wilkins, 'All we have to do is get some sort of bat or pad on it and we can run the two.' In fact Alan had a wild swing at it and missed out. I was surprised that a player of Alan's experience hadn't kept a cool head and I suspect he felt the same. He would have loved to put one over on his old county and he was desperately sorry afterwards. If only he and Grav had managed just one run, we'd have been home and dry because we'd lost less wickets and, with the scores level, it would have been our tie. Even the Man of the Match award annoyed us. Proc with his fifty must have been in contention, but Eric Russell gave it to Alan Jones for his seam bowling. Yet Jones only picked up two wickets at a cost of 44 runs. No one was more surprised than Jones himself and it just goes to prove that people who haven't played recently tend to get carried away by what happens at the end of a game. How can two for 44 win the Man of the Match award?

I left it for ten minutes before going into our dressing room, and the scene wasn't a pretty one. David Graveney was nearly in tears – he feels defeat more than most – and poor Alan Wilkins was inconsolable. I tried to lift their heads with a few words but it was hopeless. I'd have felt the same. All I could say at the end was, 'Let's go and have a drink with them and show we can at least lose gracefully.' We were grateful that the Glamorgan lads didn't gloat over us; after all, they hadn't tasted victory too many times in recent years and they'd become rather introverted. They're a far better side than they were and they've made four good signings which may have offended some of the die-hards on their committee who want an all-Welsh team. Norman Featherstone was always a good solid player with Middlesex who could score his runs, give the strike to better players and bowl presentable off-breaks; Ezra Moseley bowls seam-up off a short run and can make the ball bounce disconcertingly. Javed Miandad is simply a world-class player: I think it was ridiculous that he had to move from Sussex because Kepler Wessels was keeping him out of the side. Javed's a better batsman, a brilliant fielder and a class leg-spinner, even though he was silly enough to try seamers against us in the B & H game and got predictably slogged. But I think Alan Jones may prove to be the best signing of all. In his earlier days with Sussex, Somerset and Middlesex, people used to joke about him because he made such a noise when delivering the ball; as a fellow member of Grunters Incorporated, it seemed unfair to me to dwell on that. He's always been able to bowl fast when fit, but he needed encouragement and nursing. Brian Close gave him a hard time at Somerset but since then he's matured. He's got married, cut down on his smoking and drinking and changed his action so that he gets more sideways on, thereby reducing the strain on his back. He used to be a poor fielder as well but in the two games against us he fielded superbly. And at the moment he's almost as quick a bowler as Willis.

So Glamorgan have probably turned the corner after a bad period. Mind you, I think Malcolm Nash will only select players he can control; Tony Cordle, a fine experienced seamer, doesn't appear to figure in Nash's plans and neither does that talented all-rounder, Rodney Ontong. When we played them in a pre-season friendly, Nash fined Ontong £25 for returning late to the ground after he'd nipped out to the bank at lunch time. I think that was the correct punishment but it probably turned out to be like a red rag to a bull for Rodney.

A day off on the Sunday after the two Glamorgan games gave us all the opportunity for reflection. I spent part of it watching two games of village cricket with my family at a couple of lovely spots near my home: at Hanley Castle and Malvern. I'd sooner go and watch village teams try like hell on the field and enjoy a pint afterwards than spend a day off watching a John Player League match. At Hanley Castle their skipper came over to talk to me while in the field and said everyone loved playing there because it was always a good night afterwards in the local pub, where the beer was good and strong. That's what village cricket is all about – I wonder if I'll ever play it when my professional days are over?

I kept brooding on that day off about our performances. We'd lost four important games in a week but we hadn't been beaten, we'd *lost* them all; we'd presented the matches on a plate. In limited-over cricket in particular, bowlers have to go out and concentrate as much as batsmen. We have to bowl six good deliveries in a row and say to ourselves during the over, 'Come on, make it a maiden, forget about varying the line and length.' If you don't bowl well, you have to accept it: I bowled like a drain before lunch in the Northants second innings and I admitted it, but some of our lads look for excuses. Alan Wilkins got slogged in one match when the batsmen kept playing across the line to balls on the off-stump. I told him, 'You don't have to worry about that. If the guy's gambled and succeeded, then fair enough.' What we all need is the Brian Statham philosophy: 'If he misses, I hit.' We haven't got a great bowling line-up but we must make the best of ourselves by sheer effort and mental application. But our batsmen are just as much to blame. They threw away the B & H match against Glamorgan and in the Sunday League game against Northants, supposedly the weakest bowling side in the championship was too much for us. The basis of batting in our class of cricket is that the hard graft involves making the first fifty. After that you consolidate and when you get to your century you take a fresh guard and start again. Our batsmen *must* become more responsible and realise how much depends on them.

Our chairman, Ken Graveney, said to me that young players from other clubs always look better players than our own. I don't accept that. I believe we have a lot of young talent at Bristol. And I don't blame Graham Wiltshire, our coach, either. He catches the flak early when we're not playing well but he does all that can be expected of him and makes himself available to any player who wants his help. But in a match, the pocket in your flannels isn't big enough for him to climb into and whisper, 'Play that stroke to that ball' when necessary. You're on your own then and it's all down to ability and character. Poor Graham dies the death when he sees players he's coached failing to deliver the goods out in the middle. He's a good all-round coach and he would have been out on his ear a

22

long time ago if this wasn't the case.

The press will be on our backs shortly and the selection committee will have to resist pressure to overhaul the side. Our losing streak may go on for three months and it will only change when the senior players in the team start to play with the responsibility that their wages justify.

On to Hove to play Sussex in another Benson and Hedges match and another game we threw away, this time by nine runs. I played, even though not fully fit. After the third delivery I was back to square one again and it hurt like hell. Somehow I managed to bowl tightly and finish my eleven-over stint with a good analysis. I finished hobbling, but I got great support from the players and from the umpire at my end, Lloyd Budd. Lloyd almost counted me down in balls to go before the end of my stint, and he kept saying, 'You're bowling bloody well, keep going,' which I thought was tremendous. I only bowled at half-pace but I was pleased with my performance, even though I knew I'd be out of the next few games as a result. It didn't do any good, though – we blew it again. The total was well within our reach but Proc and Zed got out at the wrong time. Zed was playing particularly well and all the fielders were pushed back to the boundary, so there were plenty of ones and twos available, yet he gets caught on the ropes going for a big hit. Unprofessional. Then Proc went in at number 4 after asking my advice; I told him he should bat at 4 because he was the best player left and it would give him more time to play a long, decisive innings. Sussex brought Imran back to try to get Proc out. He'd already bowled five overs and they obviously wanted to hold him back for another spell at the end, so we reckoned he would have only a couple of overs at Proc. The first ball at Proc pitched halfway down the wicket and he hit it straight to cover. We never wanted more than five an over yet we cocked it up.

I didn't win the Man of the Match award, nor did I expect to. But I was amazed when it went to Tony Pigott, the Sussex fast bowler. At the ceremony the adjudicator, Les Ames, said, 'Well it hasn't been a day for bowlers but I'd like to thank Lester Piggott (sic) for a magnificent spell of bowling.' His figures were 3 for 62 off eleven overs, and two of his wickets came in the final flurry. To me the only candidate was Gehan Mendis for his hundred; he paced his innings superbly. Mind you, I was amazed at the way he and Imran played my last over. I was on my knees and there for the taking when Imran had a word with Mendis just before the over. Mendis took a leg-bye off the first ball and I said to Lloyd Budd, 'You watch this. Imran's got me lined up now, he'll try to take me apart.' Lloyd said, 'No, he won't,' and he was right – he just blocked five balls in a row. I found out afterwards what Imran had said to Mendis: 'Just block this over out and then he's finished his spell.' A great compliment to me, but I couldn't understand the tactics. After all they only won by nine runs and he would have got some stick from his captain if my last over had proved decisive.

Apart from the result and the food (a pork pie salad with the pie looking about six months old) I enjoyed the trip to Hove. I always like seaside crowds, there's a warm, appreciative feeling about them. It's a good, bouncy wicket at Hove, ideal for strokeplayers and for bowlers who want to do more than just defend. Arnold Long has done a good job down there as captain; one of his best moves was to bring Stewart Storey down from the Oval as coach, because he's got a lot to offer. But what really makes me laugh about Sussex is that they're bewailing a huge loss in their last financial year, yet they continue to employ all these overseas players. Imran Khan says he only wants to play limited-over cricket because of the strain involved, while Garth Le Roux is apparently only going to play three-day cricket. Javed Miandad, a world-class player, was kept out of the side and had to go to Glamorgan, while Gehan Mendis was sent home from an away match last season after speaking his mind about the overseas players getting so much more money than the others. It doesn't make sense to me – from what I saw of Mendis, he's worth his weight in gold. In a few years time, when the regulations on overseas players are much tighter, counties like Sussex will regret their short-sighted policy and moan about the dearth of class English players.

The Sussex defeat meant that we'd blown our chances of getting further in the Benson and Hedges Cup, a trophy we'd picked up in 1977, when Procter did so much to get us through to Lord's. But there was no point in feeling down about it, we just had to keep battling away. Our next match, a B & H game against Essex, we won convincingly. It was a satisfying result for several reasons: we were again short of bowlers, Essex are the holders and at one stage, with Graham Gooch playing so well, we looked in for a hammering. Alan Wilkins impressed me. He was very low on confidence after being taken for 42 off his first six overs but he came back to end up with 4 for 55. Martin Stovold took a magnificent catch at cover to get Gooch, and Broad, Partridge and Bainbridge all filled in well with the ball in the absence of Brain and Procter. Then the Stovold brothers won the match for us with a mature partnership. We were understandably chuffed, although Essex rather soured things in the final over. We only needed one to win and Graham Gooch came in to bowl, doing his impersonation of Bob Willis that looks so funny first time round. Phil Bainbridge was on strike and he stepped away and called Graham something uncomplimentary. I think Phil felt Graham was taking the micky and Graham didn't react very well. His next ball was as short and as wide as he could manage; it was a wide and a no-ball at the same time and Essex all stormed off the field in some temper. Andy Stovold went to shake hands with Graham Gooch, who just turned away. Andy was particularly upset because he had roomed with Graham on a Young England tour of the West Indies. The Essex lads didn't come into the bar for a drink afterwards. Some might say that they had a long journey ahead to Swansea for a Sunday League game. Well, so had we – to Leicester – yet we had a few drinks afterwards, not just because we'd won a game at last. Perhaps we're better at accepting defeat than other sides. Perhaps we get more practice at it.

We went straight up to Leicester on the Saturday night, rather than chance a puncture or holiday traffic in the morning. Most sides prefer to travel the night before a Sunday League match, because it's nice to have a lie-in, to relax over the papers and wander down to the ground at about eleven o'clock to get ready for the two o'clock start. It didn't do us much good at Leicester, though – we lost comfortably. Again we won the toss and decided we'd be better batting than bowling under pressure, so we put them in. Although John Steele bowled his spinners well, we seem to get ourselves out more than other sides and we were never in with a shout. Our secretary/manager, Tony Brown, watched the game on the players' balcony and to his credit didn't say anything when our batsmen got themselves out to a succession of bad shots. It was

25

good to see Tony there – I'm sure his presence doesn't make the players try any harder, but I know they react favourably to the presence of a man who, after all, was our skipper just four years ago. Tony is in charge of overall team matters and he has to talk about players' contracts at the end of the season, so it's right that he should see what goes on out in the middle at away matches.

I didn't play because of my groin injury, but spent a pleasant day at Grace Road, one of my favourite grounds. Mike Turner, Leicestershire's manager, looked after me very well when I asked if I could have lunch; nothing was too much trouble for him and I was pleased to see he was looking perky again after his heart attack in the winter. This man has really worked hard for Leicestershire and I was sorry to hear that it had affected his health. He told me he really has to discipline himself now not to work too hard. Unfortunately he lives almost on the ground, so the temptation must be immense. Mike Turner should be given much of the credit for Leicestershire's present status. When I first played county cricket it was a Cinderella club with little prospects, but now the facilities are first-rate, the food is excellent and the club well deserves to be awarded a Prudential International next season against Australia. I can't work out why Mike Turner has never managed a full England side abroad, unless it's because he has ruffled officialdom on occasions with some well-chosen words. He's a former county cricketer himself, so he knows the players' instincts, he's a first-rate administrator, absolutely charming to the right people and as hard as nails when necessary. I've had some inkling of how much all this administration takes out of you by watching our sponsorship manager, Chris Coley, at Bristol. He works about sixteen hours a day on match days, looking after the sponsors, checking that everything is to their liking. Such a man must be cool, calm, good-tempered, with the ability to take a quick ear-bashing from a bore and then extricate himself with good humour and tact. Every county needs someone like that, and Mike Turner set the standards.

I had a long and enjoyable chat with Ken Higgs during the Leicester game. For years I had nothing to do with him and thought him a miserable bugger, but we now get on very well. Perhaps it's because we're both elder statesmen of the county scene. Anyway, Ken sat down and talked a lot of sense. He's now coach at Leicester and he pointed out to me the faults of young bowlers like Agnew and Taylor. Ken plays alternate games now, although the arm is still high and he's still a formidable bowler. It's good to see a man with his experience passing on his tips to the first team; too many coaches spend the bulk of their time with the second XI while under the mistaken impression that anyone good enough to play for the first XI should be able to sort out his own problems.

After the Leicester game, we had a few days before the Benson and Hedges match against the Minor Counties. Talk about the lull before the storm. This was to be the match where we recovered some of our pride by smashing them out of sight. We lost by three runs. I didn't go down to the match at Chippenham, I still wasn't fit and I didn't want to get under the lads' feet. Instead I stayed home and kept in touch with the scores on the radio and by dialling 160 to get scores that are about forty minutes old. When I heard that they'd got over 200, I thought, 'Oh no, we're going to struggle,' and when we had only nine overs left and were struggling on 167 for 7, I feared the worst. I was half-expecting a telegram from Joe Lister, who used to be my secretary at Worcester. When he moved to the Yorkshire job, I sent Joe a telegram after Durham had knocked out Yorkshire – it said, 'Congratulations on being the first,' and I thought he'd rise to the bait this time. I couldn't quite believe the result. I thought, 'That just about sums up our season,' and then I thought of the repercussions. The press would go bananas down in Bristol.

I went down to the ground the next day for a fitness test on my groin in a quandary. What should I say to the lads who were humiliated the day before? If I said, 'Hard luck, lads,' their faces would probably be as long as fiddles, whereas if I ignored the result, they might think I was privately gloating, which wasn't true at all. I decided to say nothing and concentrated on getting fit. I felt sorry for the captain because he was facing the flak from all sides. He will always admit that he's as much to blame as anyone when discussing the shortcomings of our batsmen in team meetings. But honestly, you could make a tape of Proc's speech at every team meeting – the sentiments, although absolutely the right ones, are always the same and yet they don't seem to sink in. Our batsmen still get themselves out. I'm a limited player but I hope I give a hundred per cent all the time, yet our more gifted players in the side seem to have lost their hunger for the game. Sadiq has played badly and isn't getting the time to play himself back into form during limited-over matches; Zed is scoring pretty seventies but isn't going on to big hundreds. Proc is struggling with his fitness and he isn't compensating for his lack of bowling success with the bat. Somewhere along the line, our top players will have to realise it's not a God-given right to play for Gloucestershire. I hope it never happens that they will be replaced by lesser cricketers, but it might have to happen.

Next stop, Taunton for the traditional Bank Holiday fixture. I was fit and celebrated my return by getting 2 for 134 as we were thrashed out of sight by Botham. Honestly, though, I didn't bowl all that badly. I got two wickets in two balls in the morning and Gavaskar played and missed a lot. I had an amusing little set-to with Gavaskar: I beat him three times in a row, including an edge that didn't quite carry to slip. When he got a bat to the next ball, I stood there and clapped him sarcastically. To the next ball, he got right behind the line and played the perfect textbook defensive shot and said, 'Is that correct enough for you?' Honours even and we smiled at each other.

But Botham put everybody else in the shade. He just stood there and smashed us. The boundaries were so ridiculously short that he could mishit for six – and he did. With the straight boundaries no more than sixty yards long, it was very difficult for a spinner to operate against Botham and David Graveney went for 55 in his first three overs, although he stuck to his task gamely. Between lunch and tea Botham made 182 and although it wasn't a classical knock, it was still a privilege to be there. In this mood he is vulnerable, especially if you manage to get him fretting with a couple of tight overs, but his power and timing are devastating. He quietened down when he got near his double century and the old arms went up when he reached it, but he could easily have got a triple hundred. We were on our knees and there for the taking in the heat but he holed out on 228. After he got his double hundred my mind went back to the day in 1949 when Jack Robertson of Middlesex became the last man to score 300 in a day in England. It was at Worcester and I watched that innings, aged eight. I said to Proc, 'I wonder if I'm going to see it twice in my lifetime?' and he agreed that it was on. But then Botham

28

got himself out.

It was interesting to compare Proc and Botham as batsmen during this innings. Botham bludgeons the ball with a very heavy bat, whereas Proc is more textbook; he can get inside the line of the ball and hit it over cover when going well. He'll also look at the field and work out where he can get his runs, while Botham will back himself to clear the field by sheer strength and timing. Procter's footwork is better, yet Botham picks the ball up beautifully off his legs and his straight driving is thrilling. Proc is a more controlled hitter, yet on this occasion I fancy he would have made about 140 and then got out, rather than a murderous double hundred. On the whole, I rate Procter the better batsman.

After Botham's assault we had time for one drink, then into the car and up the motorway to Old Trafford for a Sunday League game – just what we needed after a long day in the field. In my car were three bowlers who'd gone for a hundred each that day (myself, Partridge and Wilkins) plus our scorer who would no doubt inform us of our figures if requested. The mood was surprisingly good in the car, even though we'd fielded to the highest-ever total in the 100-over game. There was no point in getting down-hearted, we had to keep hoping the tide would soon turn and we would begin bowling sides out.

We lost the Lancashire match, again by bad cricket. By the thirty-seventh over they needed 24 runs to win in the last four overs. I had bowled tightly and the plan was for me to bowl the thirty-ninth over. I suggested to Proc that the crucial over was surely going to be the thirty-seventh, not the thirty-ninth, but he brought David Partridge on for the thirty-seventh and they took him for 14. So my last over, the thirty-ninth, was academic.

It's always a pleasure to play at Old Trafford. The facilities are good and that warm-hearted crowd not only get behind their own side but give generous support to good cricket from the opposition. I think Jack Bond is doing a good job up there as manager: he's giving the skipper, Frank Hayes, all the support he needs and the side is developing. Bernard Reidy hits the ball very hard and he's picking up wickets with his left-arm seamers, Jack Simmons is a fine, bread-and-butter cricketer, Peter Lee and Willie Hogg are a very good bowling combination when fit and Mick Malone swings the ball skilfully and bowls a good line and length, as he must do because he's not all that quick. David Lloyd is a very good player of fast bowling and he chose that day to celebrate his return to the England fold by playing a superb innings against us.

The England squad for the two Prudential games against the West Indies was the main source of discussion on the drive back to Taunton. I thought the selection of David Lloyd was a very wise one (although I was proved wrong a few days later when he batted badly against pace) and my immediate reaction to the selection of Somerset's Vic Marks was, 'Botham must need a driver.' I don't want to sound dismissive – after all, I've said several times that Marks is a good, intelligent cricketer who could achieve international status – but it seemed too early to pitch him in. England always seem to get forced into picking batsmen and bowlers who aren't specialists in their particular field. We tend to pick bowlers who'll possibly get a few runs against world-class opposition. I felt sorry for Geoff Miller; he's been part of the England set-up for a while and now he's discarded in favour of Marks, who is not as good an all-rounder in my opinion. Miller's got over 800 runs in Test cricket and taken over forty wickets and he's never let them down in the face of scepticism about his bowling ability from both his England captains, Mike Brearley and Tony Greig.

When will the England selectors realise that Test cricket and one-day cricket are totally different games? Peter Willey should always play in the limited-over stuff and possibly Wayne Larkins. Tavare gets picked for the one-day stuff, even though he's basically a three-day batsman because he just doesn't score quickly enough. I would pick Robin Jackman for the Prudential games; he's short of class at Test level but he's bowling as well as any Englishman at the moment. He takes wickets regularly, is a great competitor and can get runs.

Anyway, that's England's problem. Gloucestershire had enough problems trying to save the match at Taunton. We managed it, thanks to a gritty hundred from Hignell and at last a long innings from Zaheer. When he plays the right way, he looks so good. The pressure was on our batsmen, Somerset were crowding us because they were so many runs ahead and we just had to play naturally, rather than get stuck in a defensive rut. The real character innings was played by Hignell. It was his first three-day game back after his broken nose and he grafted all day long in his characteristically awkward fashion. He must break a bowler's heart by the way he gets into such awful positions, but he gets everything behind the ball. He gets very square-on against the spinners, but he does this so he can focus both eyes on the ball and really watch it come onto the bat. So if the ball turns late he can make a late adjustment or let it hit his pads, knowing he won't be out lbw. With his crab-like stance he tends to miss the ball by a mile when he makes a mis-judgment but then, out of the blue, he'll hit the ball a long way by dint of his natural sportsman's eye. Higgie makes the most of his resources and if all our side had his application, we'd be better off.

In the end, the Somerset game was an enjoyable one and it was nice to see our side's true character come through in saving the match after such a terrible mauling on the first day. The crowd are always good for a laugh down there – they took the micky out of us over the Minor Counties result and called me Grecian 2000's Bristol representative because of my grey hair, but I thrive on banter like that. It's nice to hear a crowd get involved in the game rather than sit on their hands. Unfortu-nately the facilities aren't the best at Taunton; they're building a new stand which will be ready next season and the secretary had put up a notice in the dressing room, apologising for the poor facilities and promising us a palace in comparison next season. I was impressed with one thing, though: all the daily papers were in the dressing room, courtesy of a local news-agent, including the *Sporting Life*. They're the only county to do that and it's clear that sponsorship down Somerset way is really thriving.

The poor facilities gave us a chance to get one up on Somerset on the final day. Botham had stuffed us on the first day by running their bath, so that the boiler couldn't cope with another hot bath in the same evening. When we trooped off, footsore and weary after chasing the ball all day, we weren't chuffed to find cold water and nothing else. So I decided to get our own back on the final day. I told our twelfth man to run our bath at three o'clock, so that it would still be warm when we came off the field later in the afternoon. Botham then signalled to his twelfth man to do the same and a few minutes later he came out onto the field to give his skipper the doleful news –

31

cold water for England's captain. I enjoyed that and he hadn't done enough to warrant a hot bath anyway. Alec Bedser had asked him to prove his fitness to bowl on that final day and he only sent down four overs of medium pace, finishing up with off-spinners. He didn't look fit for a long bowling session against the West Indies and over a beer, he told Proc and me that he wasn't too pleased with Somerset for bowling him early in the season when his back was playing up. He felt he shouldn't have had to bowl in 'nothing' games, so that he could get a chance to rest his back.

I like Botham; he's a confident young lad, but there's nothing wrong with that. He didn't gloat and crow about his double hundred in the bar, he was quite matter-of-fact about it. I'm not sure if he'll be a success as England captain in the near future but he will do well eventually, I feel. Despite outward appearances, he does think about the game and he will ask for advice. He must have known he was in with a chance of the captaincy on the last tour of Australia when Brearley said he wouldn't tour again, and Botham would have kept his eyes and ears open after that. He's bound to have learned a lot from Brearley by standing beside him at slip; since I've been appointed senior professional, I've found myself watching Proc's manoeuvres on the field. I ask myself if I would have done the same and tell myself I made a wrong assumption about a certain player's strengths. I'm sure Botham has been doing the same for some time and at Somerset he can learn a lot from Brian Rose, a sensible, unruffled skipper who listens to players like Derek Taylor. Mind you, I don't quite know how long the England captain will enjoy being skippered by Rose.

After Taunton we faced a little jaunt of 160 miles up to Leicester for a championship match, so we'd been driving Friday, Saturday, Sunday and Tuesday night. After a time it becomes a state of mind – if you let it bother you, you'd get frightened to death just thinking about the mental and physical strains on an athlete. I do have some things to pass away the time, though, my cassettes, my TV and the car radio. My choice of music (Boney M, Barry White, Dawn and Suzi Quatro) doesn't go down too well with trendies like Partridge and Wilkins but I'm doing the driving, so they have to grin and bear it. The six-inch telly is useful; it runs off the cigarette lighter and gives my passengers hours of innocent entertainment while I plough on behind the wheel. I take it with me when I'm a passenger in other cars, and sit in the back seat and watch the horse-racing. It doesn't seem to improve my luck with the nags, though.

We all hoped the honourable draw at Taunton would mark the turn of the tide but to be honest we had the worst of the draw at Leicester. I bowled a long spell before lunch on the first day and picked up four wickets. I was particularly pleased with the one that bowled Chris Balderstone. It turned him round and opened him up a little and did enough to beat the edge of the bat and hit off-stump. If only Proc could get properly fit to bowl! Then we could start bowling sides out again. What worries me is that by the time he's fit, I'll be knackered and then he'll lack support at the other end.

Leicestershire are an interesting side to play against because they have so many spinners. And they have variety of spin – Steele bowls his left-armers flat, Balderstone tosses it up, Cook can bowl either brand, Birkenshaw flights his off-breaks and Paddy Clift can bowl flat off-spin if necessary. Young Nick Cook shaped up well; he bowls like Edmonds and got the ball to turn more than anyone else in the match. He bats capably and is a good short-leg fieldsman. They're also a side of characters. Men like Clift and Davison are as straight as a die and they enjoy a drink and a laugh after the game. Their local pub is almost on the ground and the landlady there has a bit of a soft spot for Gloucestershire. She always looks after us very well and lays on some tasty grub. One of my favourite characters at Leicester is Ken Shuttleworth. We've known each other for years – I suppose fast bowlers make a habit of talking to each other – and I've always admired his darts ability. He's an absolute crackerjack with the arrows; in the winter he won a holiday for two abroad and he plays for Lancashire. I remember playing darts with him at Gloucester for three days in a row when it rained all the time, and he stuffed me out of sight.

On the way home from Leicester on the Friday night I caught the final overs of the second one-day international. I was delighted to hear that Botham won the game for us, although I was amazed he managed to score so freely against Garner and Roberts. His eye is so good that Garner's yorker only needs to be slightly astray and he can pick it up early and hammer it. But one victory in a one-day match is nothing to get too excited about. There's a huge gulf in class between the two sides and I wish Botham all the luck in the world. I just hope England will pick specialists, not 'bits and pieces' players. I was very pleased to hear about the resurgence of Bob Willis; only another fast bowler can appreciate what he's had to go through to get himself match-fit again. Many of us, including me, had written him off after the Australian tour and although other county players had told me he was getting back to his best, I didn't believe it until he bowled so well against the West Indies. I just hope he can stay fit, because it's great to have a fast bowler of your own to dish out the treatment.

So the month ended with Gloucestershire reflecting on a dreadful playing record – Played 11, Won 1, Drawn 2, Lost 8. We were knocked out of the Benson and Hedges Cup, including defeat by the Minor Counties. Between 3 May and 14 May we lost five matches in a row and then conceded the highest total so far in the hundred-over limit for the county championship. We have just twenty-six points from five games, and in the John Player League, we've picked up nothing at all from our three matches. But we're not as bad as our record suggests; morale is good, players aren't sniping at each other yet and we're all hoping that the captain can soon find the spark to inspire us. With just a little luck in the treatment room and on the field, we would still be in the Benson and Hedges Cup – after all, we lost three times by one run, three runs and nine runs. Yet I know we have to make our own luck.

Just one pleasant task I had to perform at the end of May, a reply to an honour from St Andrew's University in Scotland that literally bowled me over. It came from the Indoor Corridor Cricket Association at the University and they'd decided to appoint me as their Honorary President; I'd been elected by a majority of seven to one with one abstention over a Mr Kenneth Higgs of Leicestershire. The letter described indoor corridor cricket as 'a quasi-religion which involves a squash ball of gruesomely variable pace and bounce, a plastic beach mat, mega-long-hops, the occasional kitchenette, plenty of nicks and a perpetually humid atmosphere that favours the bowler who keeps plugging away there or thereabouts and is always looking to do a bit.' Ah, hence the choice of me or Ken Higgs – or are we the only ones in the county championship to 'do a bit'? Anyway, the Hon. Secretary and Returning Officer

34

continued, 'I hope that you will be so kind as to accept the position which carries with it absolutely no responsibilities whatsoever except a letter of delighted acceptance and permission to use your name when recruiting new members. The term of office is one year, whereupon you will become a life member which will entitle you to absolutely nothing, except our veneration, which you already possess.'

The letter was circulated among the other members of their Association, including (mysteriously enough) 'Moira the Cleaner'. I decided to accept graciously and write back to Moira the Cleaner, saying that it was something I clearly deserved and that to mark my appreciation of such an honour, I was prepared to make a nil donation to the Association's fund. Well, you've got to encourage them, haven't you?

June

Sunday 1 June proved the old adage that a week's a long time in cricket. In the previous eight days we'd been slaughtered by the Somerset batsmen, badly beaten by Lancashire in the Sunday League and had the worst of the championship draw at Leicester. But the first day of June brought us our first victory of the season in the John Player League, and a comfortable one it was, too. We all bowled tightly and our fielding was much better. Our total wasn't that impressive, but Gooch and Lilley made a mistake when they opened for Essex. They tried to block against Procter and myself, hoping that they'd cash in against the support bowlers. They just couldn't raise the tempo and at one stage it looked as if they wouldn't get past eighty.

We needed that win and it was doubly pleasing that it came against a side that's been particularly good in one-day cricket. It's up to us to capitalise on that performance and forget our dreadful start to the season. The young players in our side have never experienced success for a prolonged period of time and it would be nice to see how they react to a good run. We could do with better weather, though. Our first championship game of June, also against Essex, died the death after we lost the first day completely. This game was played at Gloucester, which is not a good ground for me personally (I find the wickets too low and slow) and a bad one when it's raining. At a place like Bristol you can play squash or get in the gym and work off the frustrations of watching the rain fall down, but the small grounds like Gloucester just don't have the facilities for that. So we all went through our little rituals: the Essex lads kept to themselves and played cards while our main card school involved myself, Alastair Hignell, David Graveney and scorer Bert Avery. As relief from that Hignell will try his hand at backgammon or *The Times* crossword while Graveney will get stuck into his accountancy books. He takes his finals in the

36

winter so whenever it's peaceful and he doesn't feel the urge to win a few quid off me, he'll get in a quiet corner and work. Andy Brassington, always the most cheerful of players, will walk around singing, cracking jokes and telling us it's better than working down the pit. The overseas players use the time to catch up on their mail and occasionally I'll flex my fingers and have a game of darts with John Childs. The sponsors' tents are always available when it's raining but you can't really go into one and have a drink if there's a chance of play, so it's just a case of killing the time.

In fact the only person with anything positive to show from that first day of inaction was M. J. Procter. He bet all our team that the British Lions would lose the Rugby Union Test against the Springboks that afternoon. I dutifully wrote down all the names and the stakes on a pound note – including mine for a tenner – and with the Lions conceding a try in the last minute, Proc cleaned up to the tune of £67. Still, any side that scores five tries against one deserves to win.

Proc wasn't quite so lucky in his timing of a declaration when we finally started the match. He carried on batting too long when we got stuck on 160-odd. Proc wanted about 250 but we took far too long to get up to 200. Keith Fletcher had a few things to say about it and they opted for batting practice. Denness and Gooch opened with a big partnership and both looked very impressive. Denness was very polished and cool and Gooch got a powerful hundred. I think he'll become a high-class player; he presents the maker's name to the bowler, picks the ball up rapidly on his leg stump and hits the bad delivery very hard. I hope he plays the same way against the West Indies because he can disrupt their rhythm by taking the attack to them. With Boycott sealing things up at the other end, there's no reason why we can't get good starts against the West Indies. And if Gooch gets through that psychological barrier of his first Test century, he should go on and make big hundreds.

The wicket turned on the final day of the Essex match and a lunch-time chat in the dressing room with Andy Brassington might possibly help our spinners do themselves justice for the rest of the season. Ray East had bowled his left-arm spinners very well for Essex but Childs and Graveney weren't bowling out Essex. I said, 'It's because our lads bowl a different line to anyone else. On a turning wicket, the opposition always seem to bowl middle and leg, so that the left-arm spin will threaten the right-hand batsman's off-stump. But our lads bowl middle and off, turn it too much and miss the edge of the bat by a long way.' 'Brassy' agreed, and by a coincidence Tony Brown also had a word with the skipper. After lunch, Childs got six wickets.

Two things happened in that Essex innings which proved that figures can lie. Graveney bowled just as well as Childs, yet he had six catches dropped off his bowling while Childs picked up all the wickets, and Brassy took three stumpings even though he didn't keep wicket up to his usual standard. In the modern game, three stumpings in one innings are almost a collector's item but because Gloucestershire has a long tradition of spin bowling, our keeper will get more work standing up than many other county keepers. Brassington is an old-fashioned keeper in the sense that he's concentrated on learning his craft at the expense of his batting. He's a specialist rather than a 'bits and pieces' keeper but his confidence was rather low after the first month and one of his missed stumpings in the Essex game was very surprising; Gooch was stranded a long way down the wicket and Andy, in his enthusiasm, snatched at the ball before it passed the stumps. I can understand his reaction – you see a player like Gooch yards out of his ground, the ball takes an eternity to come to you and you feel you have to do something, rather than just wait for it. But Andy was furious with himself.

So the Essex match petered out into a dull draw and it ended on a rather sour note for us. Proc was furious at our missed catches on the final day and he ordered fielding practice at Bristol for the next day, which was a scheduled day off. Six of the side were due to play in the seconds, so Proc said that the remaining five – himself, Brain, Sadiq, Zaheer and Stovold – should report to Bristol at 9.30 am for fielding and catching practice. I thought that was daft, especially as Proc had a bad back and Andy Stovold had ankle problems, which would leave just three of us. When asked, I gave my opinion on the matter to Tony Brown and we discussed it with Proc at the end of the game. I think Proc felt I was being lazy but that wasn't so; as an opening bowler required to bowl about a thousand overs a season in all competitions, I thought it was important

During the 1980 championship season, the Gloucestershire bowlers were savaged by two men who reached superb double-centuries – by Ian Botham, who scored 228 for Somerset at Taunton, and by Worcestershire's Glenn Turner, who made the same score but remained not out. Here Botham hits one of his many sixes (right), while Turner (below) chops the ball away, watched by our wicket-keeper, Andy Brassington, during his innings at Worcester.

Mike Procter leads out Gloucestershire after tea on the first day of the West Indies match with the tourists in trouble. A couple of hours later Joel Garner had scored his maiden first-class century and the tourists were off the hook. Left to right: Phil Bainbridge, Alan Wilkins, Zaheer, Chris Broad, Procter, Alastair Hignell, David Graveney.

Action from the West Indies match. Mike Procter tries to deal with Andy Roberts, one of the world's most consistent and dangerous opening bowlers.

Faoud Bacchus somehow escapes being bowled in our game against the West Indies, and my reaction speaks volumes.

for me to get my feet off the ground and rest up whenever possible. It wasn't worth the club forking out £8 for my petrol money to travel down to Bristol for fielding practice with two others. I dropped a catch in the Essex game but I still felt that taking forty in a row in practice would have no bearing on how I'd shape up to a catch in the next match. In practice you are expecting the catch and you know from where the ball's coming but in match play it arrives at the most unexpected times. To me the best policy was for us all to get away from cricket for a couple of days and try to forget that bad fielding display. I don't think Proc was too happy that I gave my views on the matter to Tony Brown, but I wasn't being sneaky because my opinion as senior professional had been asked for and I had given it. Proc knows that he'll get any backing he needs from me but first we have to discuss things.

As events turned out, I wouldn't have been able to make the fielding practice anyway. I went down with enteritis the day after the Essex match and spent three days in bed, feeling sorry for myself. For the first two days I didn't get much sleep because I was sweating a lot, and then the doctor found out I'd been given the wrong tablets in the first place. I felt as if I'd wasted three days, especially when Tony Brown rang to say that Procter was injured and out of the next game and that I'd skipper the side if fit. But the doctor said I was too weak and so I missed out on one of my ambitions – to captain a side in a county championship match. I wonder if that chance will ever come again?

So I missed the Northants match, which we lost comfortably, and the Sunday game against Kent (ditto), but at least I managed to watch a great test match at home. I was really pleased at the way Bob Willis came back and proved us all wrong; his effort, line and rhythm were superb. I just hope the supreme effort of it all hasn't taken too much out of him. I felt very sorry for Gower when he missed the catch off Roberts near the end of the game. It was a wicked one to judge and I wonder if it passed through his mind as the ball came over his shoulder that the result hinged on that catch? But if Hendrick had caught Haynes earlier, I believe England would have won. Botham made the point afterwards that the ball is difficult to see at certain heights at Trent Bridge and that must have been the case for Hendrick, because you don't often see a slip fielder of his class take a possible catch on the wrist. Normally he'd get both hands to it. I thought Andy Roberts did a great job for his side, with bat and ball. He's got a great temperament and he never seems any different whether he's playing cricket or standing at the bar – he just looks straight ahead without any expression on his face. A few years ago he would slog across the line, but now he seems to pick the right ball to hit and he's a great man in a crisis.

England lost in the end by two wickets and now I can't see them winning a test. Our best chance has gone because the West Indies were a little rusty, Viv Richards alone looked as good as ever and Willis surpassed himself. I was very surprised that the Trent Bridge wicket favoured seam bowling (the West Indies trump card) but I suppose it's all part of the philosophy that fair play is the name of the game in England. Other countries seem to doctor their test wickets to suit the home team's bowlers, but not over here. Our strength has got to be on turning wickets but I bet Underwood won't get one this summer. On spinners' tracks the threat of their pace bowlers would be greatly reduced and only Holding, with his speed through the air, would remain a danger. I couldn't really fault the English team selection, either. Woolmer was a good choice, he still looks as if he's got plenty of time to play. Knott kept wicket very well and although I felt very sorry for Bob Taylor, nevertheless Knott is the better batsman and he'll prove it by the end of the series. I enjoyed the BBC coverage of the test, although I could do without the flow of statistical information on the screen. I was at home all the time and, unlike those who switch on for just a few minutes, I got bored with the same facts and figures. That's a minor quibble, though. The action replays are invaluable and concrete evidence that the umpire almost invariably gets it right, and the comments are very sound. In my opinion, Richie Benaud is streets ahead, with the ability to talk fluently and clearly on technical matters. I like Mike Smith as well; I played against him many times and he was always a thoughtful captain with Warwickshire and England. He never gives the players any stick but always offers sound, constructive criticisms, even when a man makes a bad mistake.

The first test was the big talking point in county cricket, if only because we had none of our own performances to discuss.

It never seemed to stop raining and on the rare occasions when play would have been possible, Gloucestershire didn't have a game. This was due partly to the fixture computer at Lord's and partly to our own inadequacies because we were out of the Benson and Hedges Cup. In all my time in the game, I couldn't remember a wetter six-week period from the end of April. You expect a wet May, but by June the weather's usually picked up and you tend to forget the early-season games that were ruined. For me it's so frustrating to drive all the way down to Bristol every day from Worcester, only to twiddle my thumbs and watch the rain fall. But more importantly, it's devastating for the club. We're ambitious, optimistic and in good administrative hands and we want to give the people of Bristol a team to be proud of – but how can we do that when it keeps bloody raining?

At least the weather gave me plenty of time for reflection, particularly during the match against Derbyshire when it rained for three days. I sat down with Bert Avery and analysed our playing record after eight games in the championship. We are joint fourth from bottom with thirty-nine points, while Middlesex top the lot with ninety from the same number of games. We are one of four counties to have lost three games. In the top twenty-five of the national averages we have nobody in the bowling section, while in batting, Alastair Hignell finds himself in fourth position with an average of 72: a false position, I agree, with players like Lamb, Miandad, Turner, Davison and Boycott behind him, but at least Higgie marks a big plus at this stage of the season. Further down the top twenty-five is Zaheer with nearly 700 runs at an average of 52 which surprises me because he hasn't so far looked very impressive, yet only six players have scored more first-class runs by mid-June. But we need more from Zed than occasional fifties, we need a string of big scores to give us something to bowl at. Procter is also struggling – he's hardly made a run in the championship and his bowling lacks edge. Perhaps the sun on his back will make a big difference, but will we see it for more than an occasional day this summer?

At least our form in the John Player League was starting to pick up and in mid-June we beat Worcestershire in an exciting match. But the margin of victory – two runs – was ridiculous and although I was pleased for the crowd, we were annoyed that we came so close to losing it. Zaheer got a hundred, Proc fifty-odd and the contrast in styles made interesting watching. Zed's job was to bat through the forty overs while Proc supplied the power, hitting the ball in places that Zed would never aim for, and it all worked out well. We started off by bowling tightly and when Worcestershire started panicking, they looked right out of the game. But Inchmore and Humphries came in and slogged a few, while Neale sensibly played the anchor man. Then Norman Gifford used his experience to scrape a few runs together and off the last ball, when they needed three to win, Alan Wilkins clean bowled Gifford and we scraped home.

It was a little hairy at the end, and some of us lost our rag a little in the closing overs – especially me. I misfielded a ball down at long-off and it went for a crucial boundary. I was furious at myself, not least of all because I was really wound up to do well against my old county. When the next ball came to me I fielded it correctly and, when some of the crowd jeered me sarcastically, I'm afraid I gave them a sign that Harvey Smith would recognise. Afterwards Tony Brown tore a strip off me: 'You are a professional cricketer and you should not react to such a situation like that.' He was right, of course, and I thought, 'What a silly thing to do in front of all those women and children.' That's the theory (and I really do believe that a professional sportsman should always remember that kids look up to him) but in practice I knew that if the same thing arose again, I'd probably react in the same way. Anyway, Proc thought it was quite amusing. I expected to get a rocket from him as well but he told me, 'That was all my fault, I shouldn't have left you out there, you should've been closer in with me, saving one and leaving the chasing to the others.' I thought that very understanding because he knew the frustration I felt. No matter how long you've played this game, you still get tensed up. You find yourself thinking, 'I hope the ball doesn't come to me, let one of the others stop it first.' In this match, I'd bowled my eight-over stint outright and I wished I could've been bowling at the finish because I might have been able to do something positive, rather than dread a misfield. And we would have lost the game if it hadn't been for two great diving stops by Hignell and Partridge; both shots by Phil Neale looked certain boundaries but somehow they cut them down to a couple. I wouldn't begin to know how to start diving for the ball but it looks great, the crowd love it and the strain on the Brain heart is irrelevant at moments like that.

In this match I was interested to observe the batting of Glenn Turner at close quarters. Since his double hundred against us at the start of the season, he'd been smashing bowlers all over the place and collecting his runs at great speed. In this match I bowled well at him and only twice did he try to get at me by running down the wicket and trying to slog me over cover. Both deliveries just missed the stumps and I thought, 'If this is the way he's been playing, he must have been going through a very lucky period.' Perhaps Glenn's played too much cricket. He certainly seems to have decided to enjoy himself and cut down his time out in the middle.

Phil Neale looked a good, sound player. He paced his innings very well. People are now starting to talk him into the England team, though I just don't know if he's got it against high pace. But he's a fine player of medium-pace bowling and – very important nowadays – a superb fielder. One man in the Worcestershire side I rate highly is John Inchmore. He's a very hard hitter of the ball and a fine seam bowler but unfortunately he hasn't helped himself over the years. He's a blunt Geordie who speaks his mind and he lets the crowd get under his skin when things like a dropped catch or a series of no-balls go against him. I like him and, with his ability, I think he should have gone further in the game.

One other moment I enjoyed in the Worcestershire match: catching my darts partner, David Humphries, in the deep. I did the same at Moreton-in-Marsh last year, which gave me plenty of leg-pulling mileage down the local, and Humpty gave me a wry smile when I did it again. Perhaps he was already thinking of the ear-bashing in store this winter.

Away from the cricket, there was one important day for me in June. It was my twin daughters' birthday on 17 June, and I took Eve and our three girls for a meal at a well-known cricketers' pub in the Worcester area. The Red Hart is run by Dick Thomas, a former committee member at Worcester; he still loves the game and his pub is full of cricketana. Mind you, I knew better than to talk too much cricket that night – none of the Brain females cares much about the game and although Eve occasionally comes to see me play and chimes in when cricket is discussed, she has her own interests and quite right, too. I've seen too many wives who interfered in a county pro's job to his detriment. I wouldn't particularly want one of my daughters to marry a professional cricketer for as Eve says, one in the family is enough. A job like mine is hard on a wife and young family. A footballer, for example, may be away for just a couple of days, but for a cricketer it can be ten or twelve days at a time. Take my case: when the twins were born in 1964, I was playing for Worcestershire against Cambridge University at Halesowen. I just had time to pop into hospital to see Eve and the new arrivals before driving down to the West Country to play Somerset. Then, eight months later, I went off round the world with Worcestershire on a ten-week tour, leaving my wife with three young children on her hands. It's all part of my job, but that's no consolation to the family.

There's always that nagging feeling at the back of a county cricketer's mind that perhaps he's not doing his best for his family by hanging on for one more season. It's a great life really, but the average pro like myself occasionally wonders just what he's doing with himself. How long can he keep staving off the day when he has to settle down to a regular job that brings him less personal satisfaction but more security? That's a dilemma that bothers me increasingly and the Lancashire game in mid-June did nothing to dispel the malaise. Mick Malone is a fine opening bowler with Lancashire who's been given a very nice incentive to do well for his county this year; he's being sponsored by a Manchester firm to the tune of £25 a wicket in the championship. Nice work if you can get it – wouldn't it be great if Brain's Breweries came from Bristol, instead of Cardiff and they did the same for me? Clubs are only able to pay their players what they can really afford, and I know we've always had the maximum that Gloucestershire can spare, but it would be nice to get some sponsors involved in the Mick Malone way. It wouldn't make us try any harder, but it would help break down the gap in salary between capped and uncapped players.

That Lancashire game was rain-affected but they had the better of the draw. The frequent stoppages meant I could watch a fair amount of the second test and that only confirmed my impression that England won't manage a win this series. We're not going to bowl them out on a flat wicket. Derek

44

Underwood will no longer have wet wickets to bowl on because they're now covered in tests and apart from that, he doesn't quite seem the same bowler. Perhaps it is because of a lack of continuous cricket this season or over-exposure to the West Indians in World Series Cricket. Botham didn't look a great tactician in this test but I think you've got to give him a whole series before judging his captaincy. I was very pleased that Gooch got his maiden test century; without him, we'd score at just about fifteen runs an hour. People talk about batting him at number 4 but with slow scorers like Tavare, Boycott and Woolmer in the top order we need Gooch to attack bowlers who won't send down many deliveries per hour. I'm afraid they just won't let us score quickly enough in a test to set up a platform for victory.

We rounded off the month with our southern tour, playing Hampshire and Surrey. It rained and rained and rained and I lost more money at cards as a result. The facilities at the Bournemouth and Guildford grounds aren't too great when you're not playing (they're both basically club grounds) but Dean Park, Bournemouth, with its marquees, is a pretty sight when the sun's shining. We had two enjoyable receptions at Guildford, one staged by the local mayor and the other by Gloucester Exiles, a band of supporters based in London who raise money for the club in various ways. Once a year they lay on a buffet evening for us and we always enjoy it. Socially, the Bournemouth match was memorable for the rarity of a Sunday free from a John Player League game. It suddenly dawned on me that a whole generation of pro cricketers has emerged who didn't know the sheer pleasure of lazing around on a free Sunday. Proc and myself are the only ones left who can recall the Saturday nights when you didn't have to climb into the car and drive 150 miles after a long day in the field. You could have a few pints with the opposition, a night out on the town and then relax next morning in bed with the Sunday papers, contemplating nothing more strenuous than a game of golf in the afternoon. As I played pool on that Sunday afternoon in our Bournemouth hotel, I thanked my lucky stars that I had played the game in a more relaxed era.

Surrey and Hampshire are having contrasting seasons. Surrey look a good, well-drilled side, with much of their success due to their opening bowlers, Sylvester Clarke and Robin Jackman. This bloke Clarke is very sharp and he can swing the ball too; he gets wickets for Jackman at the other end because many batsmen just concentrate on fending off Clarke and then try to score off Jackman. Robin's well ahead of anyone in the wickets tally and I'd love to see him get his hundred for the season, something he's never done. His biggest problem may be if he gets picked for the England squad and has to kick his heels as twelfth man. But I don't see him playing for England, even though he always seems to get wickets. At the age of 35, he's just too old.

Roger Knight is proving to be a good captain for Surrey and this season I've found myself wondering whether he would be our skipper now if he'd stayed with us a few years back, instead of going off on his travels that took him to Sussex and then Surrey. Apart from his captaincy, he's a very valuable player – a fine fielder, a useful medium-pacer who's particularly valuable in limited-over cricket and a consistent batsman. He plays almost exclusively off the front foot, yet he never seems to get himself into awkward positions against quick bowlers who try to drive him onto the back foot. His immensely long reach helps him play the ball on the rise from the front foot, where lesser batsmen would be hopping out of the way. Roger's turned Surrey into a side that seems certain to win a trophy soon, but he's also made them a more sociable team. Maybe this is because they're younger and more successful, but there's no doubt that blokes like Jack Richards and David Smith are great to play against and it is a far cry from the days when the Oval dressing room was a place of intrigue.

As for Hampshire, they've got problems – bottom of the county table and without their West Indians, Greenidge and Marshall, until the test series ends. David Turner and Trevor Jesty have both been short of runs and their new captain, Nick Pocock, is also trying to establish himself in the side. I had a long chat with Nick at Bournemouth and he's facing up to it all very well. He's never been a regular member of the team so the first thing he had to do was award himself his county cap, because you can't have an uncapped skipper as it more or less indicates that he doesn't deserve his place as a player. So Nick has had to earn the respect of his team-mates. I think he will score runs regularly and I hope his committee judge him at the end of the season, rather than make snap decisions as

Hampshire lurch from defeat to defeat.

At least Gloucestershire had stopped their slump of defeats by the end of June, and our victory over Surrey in the last John Player League game was an encouraging sign that we were getting things right at last. We managed only 133 but we dismissed them for 92, with all five bowlers doing their job properly. We've settled on a policy of batting first on Sundays if we won the toss because we feel our bowlers perform better under pressure than our batsmen. It seems to be working out and only Kent beat us in the Sunday League in June. At the end of the month we are eighth, compared with fourteenth at the start of June. Warwickshire are way out in front with thirty-two points from their eight games; we are on twelve points from seven games and part of a little clutch of sides that stretch up to twenty points (Somerset in fourth place). So we only need a good run in July to bring us into contention for bonus money for third or fourth place.

So far this season, I've been very pleased with my bowling in the Sunday League. I've only conceded 2.03 runs an over and that's more important than taking expensive wickets in forty-over matches. Bert Avery tells me that my run-rate per over is far better than anyone else's in the League; I certainly seem to be putting more into my delivery stride this year and I'm bowling consistently straight. Perhaps the lack of cricket has kept me fresh for the Sunday fray. The decision to open with Chris Broad and Zaheer on Sundays has also worked. In May, Sadiq was having trouble getting the innings moving and Broad's long reach helps him get on top of the bounce. He doesn't see too much spin on Sundays, so this weakness in his batting isn't tested. He's a confident young man and a splendid fielder and he should have a good July and August.

Alan Wilkins has also had an impressive month. An accurate left-arm seamer is something we've lacked since I've been at Bristol and we can now rely on Alan to bowl calmly and sensibly at all times. He's proved a very good bowler in the tight late stages of a limited-over game. We've got on to him to follow through a little more and as a result, he's surprised quite a few batsmen with extra pace and even an occasional bouncer. In the field, he's very fast with a strong throw. Phil Bainbridge has impressed as a bowler in June. His batting has stood still (a cracked finger didn't help) but he's added a yard and a half of pace, even though he's not very tall. He bowls a very good leg-cutter and he's got Allan Lamb and Graham Gooch with it this season. Phil's now a front-line bowler and he's given us a better balanced side. As for the other bowlers, David Partridge hasn't looked like getting many batsmen out, while John Childs has been inconsistent compared with the steadier David Graveney. We're still not getting many breakthroughs at the start of an innings in a championship match and Procter and Brain must take responsibility for that. At the end of June, I've taken twenty-four wickets in first-class cricket (average 28), while Proc has seventeen (average 25) and although we've missed a lot of cricket, that's not very impressive for us. I feel I've bowled well while Proc still seems below par – his shoulder injury has troubled him in the damp, cold conditions. And the wickets haven't suited his front-foot batting style, even though he's got himself out rather too much this season.

A glance at the averages underlines our patchy perform-ances in the county championship. At the end of the month I tried to find any of our players in the national batting and bowling averages. I found just one – Hignell, with a batting average of 50 for 554 runs. Andy Brassington, with twenty-six victims, is ten behind the top keeper, Gould of Middlesex. At the end of June we are fourth from the bottom, an improvement of one place in a month. Halfway through the championship season we still haven't won a match, yet just one victory would have taken us five or six places up the table. We're in a false position but successful county sides are built round two or three great players, supported by eight unspectacular pros. A glance at the averages tells me that none of our top-class players are consistently turning in the goods this season.

It's a shame that the only consolation I can find from the first half of the season is that we are in with a chance of getting third or fourth place in the John Player League. Our big chance now is the Gillette Cup – we've got a bye in the first round and face Surrey in the second round. We hammered them in the Sunday League and there's no reason why we shouldn't do the same again, provided we play to our potential. Wednesday 16 July will be the most important day of the season for Gloucester-shire County Cricket Club.

July

The month began with our stiffest opposition yet, the West Indies. With typically Gloucestershire irony, we at last looked a good side – against the world champions. We became the first county side to bowl them out twice and if that performance isn't bettered, we stand to pick up £1,200 from the tour sponsors, Holts Products. They eventually won by fifty-odd runs, but at one stage in their first knock we had them eight down for just over a hundred. Then Joel Garner came in and played superbly to get his first century in first-class cricket. I'd seen him bat well in tests on TV but never in the flesh. Perhaps we helped because we didn't bowl a short ball at him, partly because you've got to back yourself to get him out by pitching it up, and also because they would have retaliated in greater measure with the short stuff.

When we batted their bowlers pitched it halfway down from the start, so we decided to give them a taste of it in their second innings – and they didn't like it. I got Greenidge out early on, fending one away from his face to get him caught in the bat/pad position; then I bowled three bouncers in a row at Bacchus, who'd come in wearing a helmet, unlike in the first innings. Bacchus had a few words with me about the short stuff, yet I wasn't warned by the umpire. I was pleased to see that I could still make class batsmen hop around a bit when I let a few bouncers go and Proc, great competitor that he is, also slipped himself for the first time this season. Because he saw me bounce the ball, he had to make sure he could bounce it even higher, and all in all, the tourists didn't look too impressive. On the last morning, over a coffee with Alvin Kallicharran, I said, 'I'd love to see your first five batsmen face up to your fast bowlers.' 'No, no, no,' he replied, with much hand-waving and an alarmed look. I wonder how many test runs Boycott would make if he could bat against England's attack and Greenidge if he had to

49

face Roberts, Holding and Co.

In this match I decided to revert to the old style of tail-end batting. Like most late-order batsmen, I've become accustomed to pushing down the line, taking my batting seriously and trying to pick up runs by sensible methods. I think that's unfair on the crowd, and I remember seeing men like Jack Flavell and Reg Perks at Worcester scoring fifties by backing away to square leg and carving it for all they were worth. Of course they got rolled over many times, but it was good to watch. If I join someone like Zaheer or Procter, I shall block it and give them the strike, but if it's Andy Brassington or John Childs at the other end, I'm going to try to give the spectators and myself a bit of fun. That's what I did in the West Indies match. I came in facing a hat trick and on a 'pair' and I hit the first ball from Garner nearly for six over cover. The next two balls went for boundaries and then I was caught in the gully. It was short and sweet and I still hadn't got a 'pair' in first-class cricket. The crowd enjoyed it, too, and we have a duty to them.

The West Indies have worked hard on their image on this tour, following their troubles in New Zealand last winter. They're pretty good at signing the autograph books and they hand out sheets of prepared signatures to the kids. I get on well with the ones who play county cricket – men like Kalli, Lloyd, Greenidge and Richards – but some of the others are moody. I think some of them are very conscious of their colour and Viv Richards is the calming influence. He's a stronger person than Lloyd and I believe the troubles in New Zealand would not have happened if he hadn't flown home early because of injury.

There's been a lot of press talk about the relationship between Richards and Bob Willis after the recent third test at Old Trafford. It's rumoured that there's a feud going on between them, but the only evidence for that is the way Richards laced into Willis' bowling in the test. As far as I'm concerned, nobody in the game is taking that seriously. Quite simply, Willis bowled badly and Richards capitalised on that. You only had to watch Willis running in to bowl at Richards to see that his confidence and run-up had gone completely – and Richards isn't the kind of man to let him off the hook. But I know both of them well enough to know there's no bad feeling between them; at Trent Bridge, Willis was on top, now it's the turn of Richards. If it weren't for the fact that rain robbed the press box of a lot of play at Old Trafford, this ridiculous 'feud' story would never have been written.

The top-class opposition had brought out the best in Gloucestershire and we hoped to continue that form against Nottinghamshire, one of the best sides in the championship. It wasn't to be. They had the better of the rain-affected draw in the championship game and although we won the Sunday League match, we played like idiots. With rain interfering, we needed only 170 in thirty-six overs, yet Hignell tried to hit boundaries instead of just working the ball away for twos, and Proc kept trying to hit every ball out of the ground. In the end we won it by five wickets with just three balls to spare and the captain didn't appreciate my remark that the result didn't change the fact that we'd played like novices. I believe that the time to analyse your shortcomings is just after you've played badly and won rather than the other way round. We mustn't get carried away with the results as the total end product, we must keep learning from our mistakes and capitalising on opportunities.

We batted in true Gloucestershire fashion in the championship match against Notts, hanging on grimly at 89 for 8, hundreds of runs adrift from the asking target. With rain about on that final afternoon, the ball was turning for Hemmings and Bore but we didn't graft hard enough, Procter and Hignell excepted. I was very impressed with two of their young bowlers, Kevin Cooper and Peter Hacker. There's not a lot of meat on Cooper, but he's got good rhythm and is quicker than he looks. Hacker used to be a 'halfway down the wicket' bowler but Eddie Hemmings has got a grip of him and he now bowls slower, pitches it up and moves it about. Being a left-arm bowler, he has the advantage that he can swing the ball into the right-hander in the John Lever style as well as run it away from the bat.

Derek Randall didn't impress me too much, though. I know I might seem old-fashioned, but there seemed no reason to me why he should jump over the fence on the way in to bat, or play the left-handed sweep shot off the slow bowlers. I know the crowd were amused and I agree that most of us appear very dull in comparison to Randall, but I do think he plays to the gallery too much. And does he have to appeal quite so often when the ball beats the bat? He was at it consistently on that final afternoon, often when he wasn't fielding close enough to judge the validity of an appeal. Randall should concentrate on his batting – it's still not Test standard, in my opinion – and try to think of other ways to curb his nervous energy on the field.

I rate Notts as a side. They're so much better since Clive Rice took over the captaincy from Mike Smedley. The umpires were never too keen on Smedley because he used to go into their room during intervals and tell them what they'd done wrong. I don't think I ever saw Mike smile, and he seemed to me the archetypal dour Yorkshireman. Rice is different, a typical South African in the Procter style who leads from the front and will chat happily about the day's play over a pint. When he's injury-free he bowls as quick as anybody in the game and as a batsman, he just takes you apart when everything's going right. Next season he won't have Richard Hadlee opening the bowling with him; he told me that he was going back to New Zealand and staying there at the end of the season. He's got business interests back home, the financial rewards aren't good enough for him over here and in any case, he doesn't think he can stand up to another season of county cricket. Judging by the performances of Hacker and Cooper at Bristol, I think Notts will still be very useful without Hadlee.

I'm pleased that Eddie Hemmings has done well since going to Trent Bridge as he was in a bit of a rut at Edgbaston. He's a useful batsman (although I always bowl short at him and it ruffles him) and a good bowler who spins the ball. His one weakness is his run-up: he's not balanced enough in his approach to the wicket but bounces up to the stumps. Watch off-spinners like Pocock and Emburey, they're perfectly balanced and rhythmic. So Eddie will inevitably bowl badly on some days, but at least he's a regular wicket-taker. Another Notts player I like is Mike Harris and I felt sorry for him in this game. I think Mike has carried on for just one season too many. He used to be a very big striker of the ball but now he doesn't look anywhere near as fit. Mike was well-coached on the Lord's ground staff and, in his time with Middlesex and Notts, he's hit me for many runs. I just wish he'd packed it in last season when he scored a stack of runs, rather than hung around. The game looks much harder for him now and I hope to goodness I get out of it before anyone says the same about me.

But I'm still fit and I got the chance to prove that during the

Notts game. We were having a drink in the sponsor's tent one night when someone had the bright idea of organising a race. The usual Brain bravado took over and I mentioned that of course I'd back myself against anybody. Hemmings appointed himself bookmaker and I was on very long odds – not surprising when you consider that my opponents were to include Bruce French (aged 21) and Andy Brassington (26). But Mike Harris (36) and Mike Bore (a well-rounded 33) were also press-ganged into the race, so I felt confident enough to decline a 'yards for years' race. That would have meant me having an eighteen-yard advantage over French in a 100-yard race and that wouldn't have been fair on the lad. Anyway, the race was carried out across the Bristol ground, most of the punters' cash went on me (because the odds were so generous) and I won it, easing up. I kept telling them I'm quicker than they think – I've not much weight to drag about and the fags don't seem to bother me. I'd back myself in a 'yards for years' race with anyone on our staff, apart from Procter. That bloke just never knows when he's beaten at any sport and besides, I'd only have a six-yard advantage on him. I could see him whittling that away sharpish.

Another conversation with the Notts lads got me thinking about a less energetic subject – wickets. They've got pretty quick tracks at Trent Bridge (no doubt with Rice and Hadlee in mind) whereas our Bristol ones are on the slow side. As a result we have to hurry into our shots when we play on quick wickets, while at Bristol teams like Notts have to slow down their strokes to cater for the lack of speed. I think it's better for the batsmen to play half their games on a quick wicket and perhaps that's why hard-driving batsmen like Procter, Zaheer and Stovold haven't done that well for us this year. Mind you, I think first-class cricketers know very little about wickets, and we all resort to surmise and psychology. Time after time the Gloucestershire Brains Trust of Graveney, Stovold, Procter and Brain will gather round the wicket, nod sagely while prodding the damned thing – and then get proved totally wrong. Often we put a side in because we think the wicket will play up and it doesn't do a thing. The terrible weather doesn't give the poor groundsman much time to prepare really good cricket wickets with true bounce and lively pace, so we spend most of our time just indulging in guesswork. The batsmen are the worst; if we're in the field and one single ball happens to 'take off' and go through the top, taking a piece out of the wicket, all our batters will gather round the offending spot and worry. The bowlers will try telling them there's nothing wrong with the wicket but it's hopeless.

I'm firmly of the opinion that batsmen look for excuses. You never hear them say, 'What a bloody awful shot' when they're dismissed; instead we have to listen to stuff like, 'Good ball, that' or 'It really swung late on me'. They're never dismissed because of their own fallibilities, and always need to bolster up their egos. Batsmen seem to think they're the only ones playing this game – but then you'll always get this little bit of tension between batsmen and bowlers in first-class cricket. The batter will blame the wicket, the light, the umpire – anything but his own inadequacies – while the bowler will blame the batsmen for not giving him enough runs to bowl at.

No offence to our groundsman at Bristol but I wish our home wickets did more for the quick bowlers. This year in particular has been a groundsman's nightmare and I've thought a lot about what Gordon Prosser would have done to produce good cricket wickets. Gordon was groundsman at Worcester in my time at New Road and, in my opinion, the finest in England. He used to start rolling the wicket at the end of February – crossways, lengthways, day in, day out – until he'd got six inches of depth underneath the wicket which would not crumble and would give pace and true bounce. But Gordon left Worcester for Old Trafford and that didn't work out for him. The last time I saw him he was driving a bread van in Worcester and that's got to be one of the biggest tragedies in English cricket. If there were more Gordon Prossers around, Bob Willis wouldn't have had to labour for a decade as England's only genuinely fast bowler. It's bloody hard work opening the bowling for a long time, and although it's now part of our society that many avoid hard work if possible, nevertheless a fast bowler needs encouragement from the wicket. Why should he run up and down all day and end up knackered after labouring on a slow, spongy wicket day after day? I'm sure that's one of the reasons why Steve Oldham signed for Derbyshire when he left Yorkshire. A lot of other counties were after this good bowler but no doubt Steve realised he would get some responsive wickets at Chesterfield,

Ilkeston and Derby, rather than slog his guts out elsewhere for less reward.

One fast bowler lucky enough to have learned his trade on hard, bouncy wickets is the South African, Garth le Roux, and in our championship match against Sussex he effectively won the game for them – but it was with the bat. They only needed 170-odd to win and played the wrong kind of game by trying to grind out the runs. At one stage David Graveney had taken the first six wickets and they'd only got just over the hundred mark, but then Le Roux came in and smashed us. His height is a great advantage for batting and he's got a good idea where the ball should be going to, but it was disappointing to lose after recovering well from being bowled out for 140 on the first day. Graveney's performance was particularly good because he had a very painful ankle but he lacked support at the other end. Proc was right to keep the spinners on, even though Le Roux was smashing them; we always had a chance that he would be tempted to play a rash shot. There was no point in closing the game down but we should have won. We still can't bowl sides out twice in the three-day matches – apart from the West Indies!

There were two pleasant cricketing functions in mid-July, a charity match for the Bristol Hospitals Broadcasting Service and a John Player League game at Moreton-in-Marsh. A couple of times a year the Gloucestershire players turn out for the hospital service, which does a marvellous job with very little recognition. We went down to a club ground in Bristol for the match with all our squad on parade and although the poor turn-out reflected the Bristol antipathy towards sport, it was a good public relations exercise. The Moreton-in-Marsh game was unfortunately abandoned at tea-time because of a thunderstorm – a pity really, because we get good support from that part of the county. We'd like to play there more often, but the texture of the soil at Moreton is too loose to prepare a first-class wicket because it tends to break up and the ball turns square. I always enjoy going back to Moreton because I played a lot of club cricket there and it's nice to see so many familiar faces. I'm glad I played club cricket. Too many players go straight from school onto the county staff and miss out on games that start at 2 and finish at 7.30, with no overs limitation and everything depending on the goodwill of both captains to make a

55

good game of it. Nowadays there's too much league cricket among clubs for my liking. What's wrong with just enjoying the game?

That was a question I found difficult to answer on the night of Wednesday 16 July. We'd just been knocked out of the Gillette Cup by Surrey by the narrow margin of eight runs and for all of us, the season seemed over that night. We were near the bottom of the championship table, eliminated in the early stages of the Benson and Hedges Cup, moderate in the Sunday League and now a victim of the sudden-death nature of the Gillette, a competition we always fancy ourselves in because the sixty-over limit seems to suit our style of batting.

The Surrey match was a good game of cricket that we really should have won. We put them in on an overcast morning with the wicket faster and bouncier than the old-style Oval tracks. The feeling was that the wicket would roll out better as the day wore on and so it proved. The ball swung a bit at the start and Proc and I kept them quiet for a long time. David Graveney bowled superbly, taking 2 for 16 in his 12 overs, but Knight, Butcher and Jackman all played sensibly but they managed to scrape together 200. Surely that was well within our range? Not a bit of it – half the side went for 66. Zaheer was the biggest disappointment. He'd complained all day of a bad neck and his attitude seemed wrong – he was caught behind for just a single. We still had a chance while Proc was there; he'd batted very responsibly after a lean spell and now surely he was going to win it for us? With 72 needed, six wickets down and the asking rate at five an over, he was caught just inside the square-leg boundary, aiming for a six. Then Graveney and Partridge gave us some hope until I came in – yet again on a hat trick – with us needing 21 with seven balls to go. I scored two off my first ball, Grav got seven off the first three balls of the last over, then I took a single to give him the last two deliveries, but we just couldn't make it.

We all felt we'd let everyone down, including ourselves. I felt sorry for Proc because his all-round form had been much better in this match. He'd raised his game but it wasn't enough. There were two things we could have done after that disaster: slink off back to Bristol and spend a miserable time on the motorway, or have a few drinks with the opposition. Most of us stayed the night in London and drowned our sorrows, feeling

56

as sick as those parrots that footballers are always on about. I wasn't much company down at my local on the following day, either. Too many close finishes don't seem to be going our way this season.

The same thing happened a couple of days later in our next John Player match. We lost by one run to the leaders, Warwickshire, after we needed three to win off the last three balls with Proc on strike! How the hell do you lose a match from that position? It was a reduced-over match (thirty-two each) and we had plenty of batting to come. Proc had played majestically until Bob Willis bowled that last over. Then he tried to smash a boundary instead of working the ball quietly away and he was bowled. Even then it didn't matter, I thought. With Proc's face a picture of woe, I told him there was still nothing to worry about because the incoming batsman (David Graveney) was the most reliable man for the job. The fifth ball of the over was a good one, a fast delivery that bounced over Graveney's flailing bat. Three to win off the last ball, and two would do it because we'd lost less wickets. All their fielders had been waved back by Willis to save two runs, and only one man was out of his correct position. That man was Dilip Doshi, a fine spin bowler but no Randall in the field. If we could have asked for the ball to go to one fielder, it would have been Dilip. That's just what happened – Grav hit a superb shot towards Dilip at long-off and he picked it up at an awkward angle, threw in off-balance and Willis completed the run-out. If Dilip had been in the right place, we would have got two and won – but where did he learn to throw like that? David Graveney's comment of 'Whose bloody idea was it to play cricket on Sundays' came from the heart!

Dilip Doshi's certainly full of surprises. The Warwickshire manager, David Brown, told me afterwards that Dilip had won the Yorkshire game in the Benson and Hedges Cup in May in amazing fashion. Warwickshire needed 10 to win off the last five balls and Dilip, one of the true batting rabbits, got them with five successive drives for two to the same fielder!

I think Warwickshire will win the John Player League. They've taken out bowling insurance cover by signing up John Snow for the Sunday matches and the Gloucestershire game was his first match for them. A lot of people thought Warwick-shire were being cynical by signing him in mid-season but I

don't blame them. The Edgbaston crowd isn't the most tolerant on the county circuit and I can understand the committee
wanting to win a trophy this season to give them breathing
space while trying to put things right in the championship.
Snow's still a useful bowler, despite three years away from the
county scene; his arm's lower, but he knows where he's
bowling. With the bat, he hasn't lost the knack of playing
sensibly and picking up the runs here and there. Apart from
all that, his presence will surely add a few more on to the gate.

Warwickshire aren't the best side, nor even the most
talented team in the Sunday League but I think they'll win it
because they play to their strengths. Batsmen like Amiss,
Humpage and (after the West Indies tour finishes) Kallicharran can win forty-over games off their own bats while I was
very impressed with two of their young batters. David Smith
clearly models himself on Amiss, his opening partner, and he
really has got weight of stroke. Andy Lloyd's an under-rated
player who gets runs even when he's not playing very well. I
first played against Andy some years ago when he turned out
for Shropshire and he also came down to Worcester for a trial.
He's always been a happy, confident lad with the knack of for-
getting about the previous ball. In this game at Edgbaston, I
did him three times running outside the off stump and each
time he just looked up and smiled that infectious grin.

Above all, Warwickshire's fielding is in a class of its own,
and that's vital on Sundays. Willis seems to be able to keep
himself, Amiss and Doshi away from the firing line in the field
by simply moving everyone around, and the others are superb.
Phil Oliver, Anton Ferreira and David Smith have lost a lot of
weight and they throw themselves about like goalkeepers. But
the star is John Claughton, a young lad who's making his way
this season after looking out of his class in previous years. He's
an absolutely magnificent fielder, judging his dives and inter-
ceptions uncannily. The fact that he's got a bad knee and has to
wear a brace during a match only makes him more remarkable.
While Proc and I sat watching him save countless runs in the
field, we turned to each other and smiled the same thought:
'It's a young man's game now, mate!'

But Proc can still do his stuff with bat and ball, despite his
indifferent form, and if that competitive instinct of his gets
warmed up, he'll normally deliver the goods. That's something

58

the England captain found out a couple of days after the Warwickshire game. Proc took on Botham in a single-wicket competition at Bristol and, for the second year running, 'Both' was beaten. I went down to watch with some mates from Worcester and it was great entertainment. Each bowled ten overs at the other, Dilip Doshi bowled the other ten, and the fielders were provided by local club cricketers with Andy Brassington keeping wicket. Doshi bowled a containing middle and leg line and seemed to bowl better at Botham. Perhaps Procter's footwork is better. I think Botham should have won but he got himself out a lot in his twenty overs. The crowd was good (about 4,500), the atmosphere good-natured and Proc picked up £1,000 and Botham £250 for three hours work. I wish I could bat like them. I'd be a rich man by now.

Another enjoyable match to watch in July was the Benson and Hedges Cup Final, although I was amazed that the BBC cut away from the excitement to bring us turgid shots of gymnasts from the Olympics before going back for the last couple of overs. I was very pleased to see Northants win so narrowly. No offence to Essex, but they had their double glory last season and men like Cook, Sharp, Watts, Lamb and Griffiths deserve some success for years of honest endeavour. I think a left-arm spinner would make them a very good side indeed. I was impressed by the way someone always came up with an important contribution at a crucial stage in the final, a tribute really to the quiet, mature captaincy of Jim Watts. I was particularly pleased for him. He came back from retirement into a sour atmosphere after the sackings of Mushtaq and Bedi and then his wife died in the same year. Now he's going back to teaching, leaving behind an extremely talented and happy team, and that's not a bad legacy for any retiring captain.

The month ended with us up in Yorkshire and play delayed on one of the days for something other than rain – mist, would you believe, in Sheffield of all places. We lost three hours because of that and with the usual stoppages for rain, there was little elbow-room for either captain. I bowled quite quickly in the first innings, Sadiq batted well after being dropped into the second team to regain some form, but eventually it all got rather meaningless. Athey and Lumb picked up hundreds against bowlers who weren't trying all that hard on the final afternoon and the day dragged on a little.

People have been telling me for years that Yorkshire were soon going to dominate county cricket. I certainly thought that Ray Illingworth would bring that little bit extra out of them, but so far they're still flattering to deceive. Test calls don't help, but they do have gifted reserves; unlike other counties, Yorkshire seem to be able to hang onto their second-team players. I remember Ray Illingworth telling me last season that all his players had been tapped up at some stage by other counties, yet they all seemed happy to stay with Yorkshire. I suppose it's to do with inbred tradition, because when they don that Yorkshire cap they really are a breed apart. They have an air of superiority that helps psych many young opposing players off their game. But for all that, I find them good blokes on and off the field, and I hope they regain their former eminence because Yorkshire cricket has so many things in its favour.

Our bowlers got another hammering from the Yorkies in the Sunday League. We got 230-odd on a beautiful wicket, with Zed getting a hundred, but then they knocked off the runs for the loss of just four wickets and with two overs to spare. We all bowled very badly and I thought I knew why. We'd just started a new fitness programme under the guidance of our physio, Les Bardsley. Les, a former professional footballer with Bristol City and manager at Bury, got us doing some running and a few stretching exercises and then made us finish off with sprints. I think his programme is very good but this Yorkshire game was the first limited-over match we'd had since starting the new system and the bowlers were gone in the legs – the sprints finished us off and made us stiffen up. But it's a good way to teach the younger players discipline. After all, we haven't really done any concentrated physical fitness work since we started playing at the end of April, and it's good to get all the team involved. Watching John Claughton scudding around the boundary at Edgbaston made me realise that no longer can we rely on match practice to get our lads completely fit. Mind you, I'll try to get out of it when I can – after all, my bowling keeps me fit and they don't really expect me to dive around à la Claughton, do they?

Perhaps Les Bardsley's fitness programme will help us turn the corner on the field in August. Somewhere along the line we have to win some championship games. It's a depressing thought to offer an improved showing in the John Player League as the sum total of our performances so far this season. I'm getting fed up with losing games by narrow margins; if the TV cameras followed Gloucestershire around in the one-day competitions, they'd get great value for money and plenty of twanging nerve-ends. But you try telling that to the players and to the people who pick up their papers the next day and think, 'I see Gloucestershire lost narrowly again. What bad luck.' As far as I'm concerned, you make your own luck and it doesn't matter whether you lose by two or two hundred runs. At the end of July we are second bottom of the championship table, having played fourteen games, so with just eight to go, we are still without a win. Only Leicestershire and Hampshire are in the same boat. In the John Player League we are lying tenth with six games to go. A couple of wins would still put us into contention for talent money for finishing third or fourth. But consolation prizes like that aren't enough and the fact that we've hinted at our true quality is even more galling.

At the start of the season I thought our bowling would be the big problem and that our strong batting would be enough to see us through, provided our batters did themselves justice. It just shows how you can get things wrong: we've only got twenty-one batting bonus points, worse than anyone else but Lancashire, and our 'weak' bowling has seen us pick up forty-two bowling bonus points, inferior to just three sides – the top three in the table.

So far Procter's taken only twenty-nine first-class wickets (just twelve in July) and he's hardly got a run. Last year he had a fabulous August with bat and ball and I only hope he'll do the same. Without some consistency from the captain, we'll struggle to get even one victory in the championship. Andy Stovold has had a nightmare month, scoring forty-five runs in the championship, while Hignell has also struggled after a good start. Sadiq has got very down about his form; he seems to have more bad spells than most players of his class. He no longer opens the batting in Sunday League games and I wonder just what effect sitting around waiting to bat has on him. But at least he's practising hard in the nets and he's reacted well to being dropped, although he still hasn't scored a first-class hundred whereas last year he made eight.

61

Chris Broad, the man who's replaced Sadiq as opener, is the main plus so far. At the start of July he played very well against genuine fast bowlers like the West Indians, Imran Khan, Garth Le Roux and Sylvester Clarke. He plays them so well because he stands up straight and lets the ball pass by if he doesn't want to play it. He's a tall, strong lad and we've told him to go through with his shots instead of poking around. Now he gives it a real whack and doesn't get caught at mid-off very often. I first laid eyes on him when he toured Malawi in the autumn of 1978 and he looked a very good player then, although it would be wrong to judge him on matting wickets against club bowlers. He's been dropped several times in the past two seasons and always comes back a better player. In a couple of weeks the Australians are due to play Young England at Worcester and I reckon Chris Broad must be in with a chance of playing. I'd like to see how he'd shape up against Lillee and Thompson.

Alan Wilkins sums up our playing dilemma: he's in the first-class averages with twenty-six wickets at nearly 24 a wicket, but he doesn't yet believe in himself. Alan appears to settle for a couple of cheap wickets rather than aiming for all ten. It doesn't matter how many they cost, as long as you bowl sides out quickly in three-day cricket. We keep telling Alan to be more positive, that he has the ability to bowl a quick bouncer. He can summon up an extra yard of pace when he wants to and he only needs to do that once in a while, when the batsman doesn't expect it. But he seems happy with just line and length, and a third seamer needs more than that in the championship. We're just not bowling out sides twice in a match and with Proc and myself being over-bowled, we've got nothing left to polish off the tail.

As for myself, I'm happy with my bowling but not with my career. I'm worried about the future of the game and more particularly what I'm going to end up with after more than twenty years. Let's face it, I'm not going to get any better. I'm nearly forty and I don't want to bat number 5 and bowl off-spin in league cricket, while regaling everyone with stories from my past – I can just hear them now all saying, 'What's Mike Procter really like, Brian?' Several things happened towards the end of July that increased my disillusionment. I captained the second XI at Bristol and I was appalled at the defensive attitude of the Hampshire side. Mike Taylor and Peter Sainsbury were in charge of them and they never played a shot in anger on the last morning. I felt sorry for their young players and wondered what kind of state the game was getting into when a second XI game wasn't being used to increase the education of the young players.

The sight of Mike Harris struggling when we played Nottinghamshire made me wonder if I'll soon be in the same position. I've never been the greatest fielder in the world and I'm worried about becoming a passenger. As a bowler I keep going but there'll come a time when I just can't manage twelve overs on the trot and expect to come back after a break. The saddest sight I saw in cricket was at Worcester last year when Proc bounced out Basil D'Oliveira. Dear old Bas just couldn't accept that the years were catching up on him; he got 0 and 1 and couldn't cope with Procter. I shan't hang around long enough for my fellow-pros to feel sorry for me.

The travelling is getting me down, too. When we played Yorkshire at the end of July, we went to Hull on the Sunday and travelled back to Sheffield after the game. I could hardly get out of my car when we got to the hotel, and I was due to bowl the next day! Proc does his best to gee me up on the field ('Come on, Brainy, that ball's coming out of your hand like an apple') and I'll try my best for a man like him – but it's getting harder and harder.

Yet I can live with the travelling if it's all going to be worth it, but what about my financial future? I see people like Jim Foat doing a sales rep's job around Bristol, just a year after he was sacked by Gloucestershire in the season he was awarded his county cap. I read about Hampshire's David Rock packing up first-class cricket because he wants to pursue a career in accountancy and I think, 'Quite right, too.' Nobody will thank him for shelving his accountancy plans to make a serious effort at cricket where he would be paid for results, not for trying to get them. Worcestershire sacked me a year before I was eligible for a benefit and I certainly won't get a benefit with Gloucestershire because I shan't be playing in the appropriate year of 1987 (ten years after getting my county cap). But there's no rule against a player getting a testimonial, in other words a mini-benefit. You don't have to be with a club a decade to qualify for that. A lot of players ask me about a testimonial when we go round the counties and they can't believe that I've had nothing. Correction – in 1975, a testimonial for Rodney Cass, Jim Yardley and myself was organised by some Worcestershire members after we'd been sacked. We ended up losing on the whole thing.

I've had a few meetings this month with officials at Gloucestershire. Ken Graveney, our chairman, tells me there's nothing to worry about, that it will all be sorted out. Ken has always been fair and honest with me and I hope I'm worrying for no good reason. I can't keep playing much longer and certain suggestions have been made to me by other counties that there could be something in store on a managerial or a coaching basis elsewhere in county cricket. Then there's my winter job with Grasshopper Sports to consider. I enjoyed working for them last year so should I stay in cricket or chuck it all up and work full-time as a sports equipment manager? And what about my family? How will they react if I'm tempted by a coaching offer on the south coast?

I shan't go on the trip the county is making to Barbados in September if I retire. It would be unfair to the rest of the lads and I would feel out of it. And I shall want Eve to drive me back from our last match at Chesterfield on 7 September. I don't want to drive all the way up there on my own, knowing it would be terrible coming back on my own, or with mates like Bert Avery or Andy Brassington. They may be mates at the moment but it's amazing how you lose touch once you've retired.

The uncertainty over the captaincy doesn't help, either. Proc has made no secret that he's now finding the job hard going, and none of us really know what's going to happen. It may be that he'll carry on as captain for one more season, then have a big say in his successor. As I see it, the contenders are Hignell, Stovold, Graveney and – myself. They may give it to me as a short-term solution, but I'm not sure that it would work. Still, it would be nice to know where we all stand.

I'll have to make a realistic decision on my future within the next fortnight. The days are slipping by, the Barbados trip gets nearer and all the lads are talking excitedly about playing out there. I must be dispassionate about my decision and resist the temptation to go out there if I know I am going to retire. Short-term enjoyment is no longer important. I'm forty in a few weeks time and I may be entering the final month of my first-class career.

At least I've now got a rock group named after me. Have you ever heard of Public Image Ltd? Neither had I, until a boy friend of one of my daughters brought round a cutting from a pop magazine. It seems Public Image Ltd have changed their name to Brian Brain and the reason they gave was this: 'Don't know. It just sounded a lot more interesting.' Well it would, wouldn't it? I've always felt I had charisma. I'm told their punk style isn't really up my musical street but you never know, they may send me some royalties from their record sales and help ease my financial insecurity.

August / September

Tuesday 6 August was the day we'd all been waiting for this
season. We actually won a championship match, and a
resounding victory it was, too – against Hampshire by 197
runs. And in typically anti-climactic fashion, I spent that day
in bed at home, feeling sorry for myself. I thought I'd caught
the flu so I was tucked up, wondering how the lads were getting
on, when the phone rang. It was David Partridge with a
message from the captain, asking if I was going to be fit for the
next day against Worcestershire. 'How the hell should I know,'
I moaned, feeling distinctly self-pitying (something that
always comes naturally to me); then, as an afterthought, David
said, 'Oh, by the way, we've just won.'

The spinners did the damage on the final day. It's amazing,
everyone tells me that the ball turns at Cheltenham but in all
my time in the game, that's never happened. It's often been a
seamer's wicket – and the day when the ball actually does turn,
I'm in bed! The only thing that took the shine off our victory
was that it was against the bottom club, and indeed Hampshire
didn't look all that good. But we'd turned the corner and there
were some good individual performances from our lads. Chris
Broad got a very good-looking hundred, with some fine shots
off his legs, Sadiq got an unbeaten 90 and Alan Wilkins bowled
very well in the first innings. Before going ill, I'd bowled my
quickest yet for Gloucestershire. I really slipped myself on the
Monday morning when it all felt just right, and the slips went
two yards back. In the John Player League game on the
Sunday we scrambled home in a rain-affected match by two
wickets in the last over. The Gloucestershire Edge-of-the-Seat
Brigade strike again! But really we made very heavy weather of
it and we should have coasted it. All our lads took part in the
tea-time interview for BBC-2 and we found it very enjoyable.
Peter Walker, a man I'd played against many times, was the

interviewer and did his job very well in a calm, relaxed fashion. He's as good as anyone in this job and we often have a yarn about the old days when we were a gangling pair of young hopefuls. He was one of the finest fielders round the corner I've ever seen, and he got hundreds of wickets for Don Shepherd. He also did the double and as a batsman, he intelligently made the best of his resources by building his innings. A great competitor, Peter played three times for England and he wouldn't be far off the side if he was playing today.

One pleasant little moment in the Sunday game: it was John Arlott's last visit to the Cheltenham ground as a commentator and the crowd was asked to give him a warm send-off in true Gloucestershire fashion. That must have been a poignant moment for him as the applause echoed round the ground which has always been one of his favourites. John Arlott has been that rarity, a man respected by the players as much as by the public. I can't believe I'll see anyone like him again, for he belonged to a different era of cricket and I feel very sad at his retirement. Somehow Arlott's presence made you feel cricket was in good hands.

I had a nice chat with Hampshire's new opening batsman, Chris Smith, during the Sunday game. He's in his first season with them after coming over from South Africa and he's full of county cricket at the moment. He's desperately keen to learn and I see no reason why he won't prove a very good purchase. He's a curiously non-South African batsman; with no frills, he gets behind the line and plays like a solid English opener. I hope he does well, and he's certainly got the right attitude.

So we'd broken our duck in the county championship, and none of us were surprised that it was at Cheltenham. We all like playing there because it has atmosphere and the crowd get behind us. We always seem to end up with results of a positive kind in the Festival and it's a good cricket wicket. It's a pretty ground with imposing Cotswold stone buildings, and many of us enjoy walking round the boundary and meeting old friends. Mind you, the way we've batted this season, there's always a chance that numbers 9, 10 and 11 have to rush back and put their pads on, but Worcestershire's batting was a good deal more fragile than ours in the next match at Cheltenham. They just caved in against the swing of Procter and he took fourteen cheap wickets in the game with some excellent, sustained, intelligent bowling. Even though the blond hair was flapping and the gold chain, arms and legs were whirling, he didn't bowl all that quickly, but he swung it a hell of a lot. He had to go round the wicket to the left-handers to minimise the swing, otherwise he would never have got an lbw. Proc bowls well against left-handers because his natural swing is away from their bat. Six times out of eight successive balls he beat Henderson outside the off-stump. Left-handers tend to miss the ball by a long way because they play wicket to wicket, rather than at the angle from where the ball is delivered, so batsmen like Peter Denning, Brian Rose and Roger Knight often miss the ball by some distance when they're beaten outside the off peg because they're playing down the wrong line.

Procter's character really showed through in their second innings, because he was without the services of B. M. Brain on a wicket that would have suited him. I was hit painfully on the thigh when batting; there's not a lot of meat on my thighs, so any blow there gets to the bone. Paul Pridgeon was the bowler and I sat cursing this genial lad over a pint afterwards. I'm one of the few people living in Worcester who think Paul can bowl, judging by how often he's left out of the first team. He's built a little like me, but he hits the seam and as my thigh will confirm, he's pretty sharp off the pitch. He's a very fit lad and still only 26 and it's high time he was given the chance to consolidate his place in the side.

My mate David Humphries had been dropped to make way for a newcomer called Paul Fisher. He performed competently enough, taking catches that Humpty would have also snaffled, and although he's definitely a better keeper than Humpty, I can't see how he can keep him out for long because he's far inferior as a batsman. There were three batters in their top seven in this match who aren't as good players as Humpty – and I'm not saying that just because he's my darts partner. Maybe Humpty has got complacent because nobody's been pushing him for his place now, or maybe all that training to lose his excess weight has sapped his strength. He's always going to be a chunky lad and if you lose too much weight too quickly, you end up hardly able to get the ball off the square.

Worcestershire look as if they're getting old together. They need a few players aged around twenty-eight to thirty to bridge the gap between their youngsters and Gifford, Turner,

Hemsley and Ormrod. They went to pieces in both innings when Proc got Turner out and someone like a Knight, a Roope or a Radley was needed to hold things together in the middle of the order. All the successful sides have this blend of experience and youth and neither ourselves nor Worcestershire have quite got it right at the moment.

By the end of the Worcestershire match we were convinced we'd got the clean sweep in the Cheltenham Festival – and the fact that Middlesex, the championship leaders, were our next opponents, didn't matter a jot. So it proved: we played above ourselves and won, chasing 270 in 285 minutes. The hero was Procter, with an absolutely superb 134 not out, and quite honestly I've never seen him play better. Not only did he play responsibly, but for the first time I can recall, he encouraged a young player at the other end in just the right way. Phil Bainbridge had had a terrible season for someone with his potential and when he first came in, he was in trouble; but several times Proc quietly came up to him with a few encouraging words and you could almost see Phil increase in stature. Most overseas players take the same attitude as our captain to their batting partner – that a first-class cricketer should be able to work things out for himself – but I was glad that on this day he chose to talk Phil through those early stages. Just before tea, Proc played a few flamboyant shots and I said during the interval, 'Listen, just play sensibly and we've won the game.' He said that it was best for him to play his normal game but I told him that the match was ours if he was still there after another hour. So it proved and against Daniel, van der Bijl, Titmus and Selvey he played an innings I'll never forget.

Irrespective of the result, that Middlesex match was a great game of cricket. After taking Les Bardsley's advice that my thigh injury wouldn't get worse and a promise from the captain that he'd take responsibility if I broke down, I agreed to play. I took five wickets in the first innings and felt fine after a long bowl. I only ever bowl from the College End at Cheltenham, because the slope that goes from left to right at the other end seems to drag me over and unbalance me; that day, I was very happy with my rhythm and control. I got Barlow out in the usual way – caught at mid-wicket off a bouncer which he never seems to play all that well – and I bowled especially well at Brearley, turning him round, opening him up and getting him into bad positions. Brearley's still a very fine captain but I think he made two errors in this match. The wicket went very flat and I thought he would have called for a roller at the start of their second innings in the hope that the wicket would have broken up a little; after all, he had a nice balance of seam and spin to cash in on a wearing wicket. Yet he never bothered with a roller. Then on the second evening, I was surprised that Brearley and Downton didn't press on with their batting. We were a fair way behind on first innings and the order of the day was surely to get on with it. But they took ages to put on 44 for the first wicket and in all, forty-seven overs to make 158 before the declaration on the final day. If men like Butcher, Barlow and van der Bijl had had longer at the crease, their hitting could have put the game beyond our reach. It's funny how fate takes a hand, though: Procter was dropped by Brearley off a fairly straightforward chance when he'd made only 38, and another dropped catch helped us avoid the follow-on. We were 63 for 7 in our first innings when Wayne Daniel dropped a fairly easy one at long leg to reprieve Alan Wilkins, who then hit the next two balls for boundaries and we stayed in the game. But it might have been so different.

I was very impressed both on and off the field by Vintcent van der Bijl. On the Saturday evening he bowled a magnificent spell – indeed, David Evans, the umpire at his end, said it was the best spell of new-ball bowling he'd ever seen. I'd been looking forward to watching him bowl because I'd heard a lot about him this summer. I wasn't disappointed. He ran a little further than I realised and looked awkward when he was getting near to the crease, but everything's right in the delivery stride. He hits the seam all the time and never seems to bowl a loose delivery. He and Procter play together for Natal in the Currie Cup back home and I agreed with Proc that he was everything he'd been saying about him in recent years. He tends to bemuse the batsman into thinking the next ball is going to be pitched short, only to get one in the block-hole. That's how he got Proc, forcing him to play on – Vintcent loved that one. And what a super guy he is! If he bowls you a great ball and you get nowhere near it, he just grins down the pitch at you. Off the field, he's the most affable man, and very close to the West Indian, Wayne Daniel. There was no show at all about their relationship, they were just totally relaxed in each

70

On another wet day, the team horse is in the lead entering the final furlong (above) but is beaten in a photo finish (below). Left to right: Stovold, Graveney, Procter, Sadiq, Surridge and a crestfallen Brain – it was my tip.

Mike Procter was still kicking himself at the end of the season for losing the John Player League game at Edgbaston. We needed just three to win with three balls left and stacks of wickets in hand, but Bob Willis bowled Procter and we lost. 'Proc's' expression says it all.

In the same match Andy Stovold achieves that rarity in the John Player League, a stumping. John Claughton is the stranded batsman.

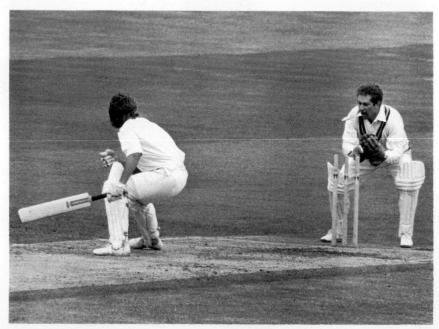

'Zed' works out where to place his few bob. Andy Brassington is in the background.

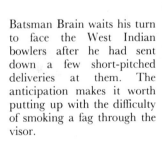

Batsman Brain waits his turn to face the West Indian bowlers after he had sent down a few short-pitched deliveries at them. The anticipation makes it worth putting up with the difficulty of smoking a fag through the visor.

Two contrasting Gloucestershire grounds: Bristol (above) during the West Indies game and Cheltenham (below), where another Hampshire wicket has just fallen during our sequence of five wins in a row during the 1980 Cheltenham Festival.

other's company and clearly there was a lot of mutual affection and respect. Now I know that sport and politics can no longer be separate entities, but I wish some of the more fanatical anti-South Africa brigade had seen how cricket had brought these two blokes together.

It was lovely to see Fred Titmus playing again. This bloke seems to have made more comebacks than Frank Sinatra, but at the age of forty-seven he can still bowl and play straight. He finds the fielding hard and was put in one-saving positions most of the time to avoid too much running about, but the bowling ability hasn't deserted him. No off-spinner could bowl the away swinger like Fred; you just couldn't pick out the one that floated gently away from the bat rather than turned in. His variation is still there and he's a master craftsman. Looking at Fred, I wonder just how long I can keep going. Certainly not till I'm 47!

Brearley seems more relaxed now that he doesn't have the cares of the England captaincy on his shoulders. He's still very much in charge out on the field but he'll have a laugh and a joke as well during the game. And although he's never been a man for the card schools, he doesn't lock himself away any more. Instead he'll stay on the fringe of the card schools, catching up on his mail but happy to join in the banter. It's ironic that he's having his best batting season for years after all the traumas he went through about his form in Tests.

My abiding memory from that Middlesex match will always concern those two South Africans, van de Bijl and Procter. It was only after Vintcent nipped in to congratulate us and wish us well that I realised I'd probably never see him again. He can't get any extra time off work to come back for another year, so he has to content himself with the fact that he was a great success in his one and only season in county cricket. If he'd come a decade ago, he'd have taught the youngsters so much about seam bowling because he's a superb, articulate talker about his craft. If he'd played test cricket, I'm convinced he'd have been another Joel Garner, getting bounce out of flat wickets and dropping in the occasional, devastating yorker. Vintcent made a deep impression on me and I think he was a great credit to the game of cricket in the 1980 season.

The other sight that will forever stick in my mind was Procter's face as he came into the dressing room after his great innings. We'd just won five games in a row at Cheltenham (three championship and two John Player League) and his expression contained all the emotions. He's not a very demonstrative man but he was as happy as a small boy with extra pocket money. I don't think he was all that pleased for himself, it was more to do with beating the top side, both in the three-day game and in the Sunday League. The Gloucestershire dressing room was a good place to be on Tuesday 12 August and even a sardonic, seen-it-all-before man like myself was talking nineteen to the dozen. There was Phil Bainbridge (normally a very quiet lad who only speaks when he's got something worthwhile to say) chattering away, his poor season a distant memory and his fine supporting innings that day fresh in his mind. We moved down the road for a few celebratory drinks at Peter's Bar (a friendly cricketers' pub where a lot of our members gather) and the mood was sweet indeed.

I think we deserved our moments of pleasure; we put a better face than most on defeat and we don't slink away without facing the opposition when things have gone wrong for us. But although we say the right things in defeat, some of us get very down when we lose badly or through our own fault. David Graveney suffers more than most because he's also got the family name to live up to; he's a happy, pleasant lad who thinks deeply about the game and when he's down, it's only too obvious. John Childs as well – one of the nicest, gentlest lads I've met in cricket but he takes bad performances very much to heart. Chris Broad shows his unhappiness in a different way: when things are going well he's a great micky-taker, yet if he's out of form or the team's doing badly, he seems incapable of seeing the funny side of things. Our two Pakistanis react differently. Sadiq feels for the side and for our collective self-respect while Zaheer is more enigmatic. It's often difficult to tell what he's thinking but I suspect he's more wrapped up in his own batting than in the team's overall performances.

A complicating factor with our lads is that we've got some very intelligent blokes on the staff, with other strings to their professional bows. Bainbridge, Broad, Hignell, the Stovold brothers and Surridge have all trained as teachers, while Graveney has his accountancy background and Partridge his degree in civil engineering. I wonder if sometimes our lads think, 'Oh well, there's always my other career' when things are going consistently wrong for them on the cricket field? I'm sure it would only ever be sub-conscious because all of them want to succeed in cricket, but I wonder sometimes if a hungry cricketer is a better cricketer? Not many are like our captain; he's a professional cricketer all the year and stands or falls by his performances. He never seems to show the strain of that lifestyle but I do feel sorry for him when we don't do ourselves justice as a side.

Within the space of ten days we'd risen from third bottom in the championship table to seventh from the top and we were even beginning to show in the national averages: Procter was eighth in the bowling list, Brassington was top keeper and Sadiq was two catches short of the leading fieldsman. There are cash incentives then for those three lads for the rest of the season, although we don't really need them to do our best. I can't really put my finger on the amazing turnabout in our fortunes, apart from the fact that it happened at Cheltenham. For some reason Gloucestershire always start badly, but by August we come onto a good run which always seems to coincide with the Cheltenham Festival. We find ourselves saying in July, 'Oh, it'll be all right, we'll soon be at Cheltenham' and by the time we came to the Middlesex match, we were convinced we'd win it. The atmosphere is just right for us at Cheltenham and it seems to bring out the best in Procter. One of these days, we'll come to the Festival near the top of the table; that's the time to put a few bob on us winning the title a month later, because we feel like supermen at Cheltenham. When things are going our way, we feel we could take on the world; the fact that we've put up the best county performance this season against the West Indians and last year against the Indians underlines the point that we seem to play better against class teams.

We still lack consistency, though, especially in our batting, which helped bring us down to earth with a nasty bump in the next match against Glamorgan. On the first day our batters kindly gave me the opportunity to play a long innings when I batted for an hour and a half to try to retrieve something. John Childs, a natural number eleven, hung around with me for a while and we added forty-odd to put some respectability on the score. Then Norman Featherstone showed our batsmen how to graft with an invaluable century, even though he didn't play very well – a fact that I can vouch for because I bowled a lot of my forty-three overs at him. But we were still in with a chance until the game was settled in the last half-hour's play on the second evening. With Procter and Zaheer together we thought we were just getting out of the wood until Zed put one straight up in the air. If they'd been together on the final morning we'd have been in control, but we collapsed from 186 for 5 to 236 all out. They needed 170 to win and they just picked us off for the loss of two wickets. We tried eight bowlers, but it was a lost cause.

Malcolm Nash got plenty of wickets for the second time this season against us and I hope I don't sound unsporting if I say he's lucky he gets the new ball – otherwise he'd end up as cannon fodder. Still, Nash has moulded Glamorgan into a far better unit than last season, although I got the impression that Javed Miandad was more in charge than the last time we played them early in May. They've got some good players: Ezra Moseley is a sharp bowler, generating pace from the same short run-up he uses in the John Player League; Javed is a superb batsman, even if his running between the wickets sometimes ends in tears (he was involved in three run-outs in our Sunday game); and Alan Jones is a fine player. I was very impressed with his judgement of the line in their first innings when I bowled round the wicket at the left-hander. The ball was swinging a lot and Alan kept padding me away when the ball pitched outside the off peg. I was waiting for the time when he misread the swing before launching into a big lbw appeal but it never came. He's a really fine, calm opening batsman, this bloke; it's amazing that he's only played once for England, and that against the Rest of the World in 1970, which has now been declared an unofficial 'test'. So now Alan doesn't even have the consolation of one test appearance and that's diabolical. If he'd played for a fashionable southern county, his cabinet would be full of England caps. He's so solid and professional – you look up at the scoreboard after a time and you think, 'How the hell did Jones get to thirty so quickly?' and then you remember how he tickled one fine for a boundary, how he guided you all along the ground past gully for another four. 'It soon mounts up' should be Alan Jones' motto, and everyone in the county game respects this unfussy, uncomplaining grafter. He's nearly forty-two as well and shows no signs of decline – I must get some tips from him about growing

74

old gracefully in county cricket. I wonder if the young pros bring him breakfast in bed, and carry his kit for him? I think I'll suggest that to some of our young shavers.

The next match was, quite simply, the highlight of my career and it will always remain so. On the face of it, the game against Kent at Folkestone was fairly routine and neither of us had much to play for, apart from our own professional pride. But I realised the only ambition that's left to me: captaining a county in a championship match. To make the occasion even better, we won.

The facts behind my big moment are predictably bizarre. Proc was struggling with a sore hip in the Glamorgan match and on the last day, David Graveney and I told him he shouldn't travel down to Folkestone because we needed him fit for the remaining games. He agreed with us and at the end of the match wished us both 'good luck' and went home to Bristol. We all set off on the long haul from Swansea to Folkestone – and my car conked out with over-heating trouble fifty miles from our destination. By the time we'd messed around and got a taxi, it was after midnight before Alan Wilkins, Bert Avery and myself staggered into our hotel. I'd left the car where it broke down and rang to ask my supplier, Lex Mead, to look after it for me; it was ironic really, because I'd asked Lex for a change from my Marina Estate as I knew a long drive was in store. He had given me a 3.5 Rover Automatic, which went beautifully until it over-heated! Anyway, the captaincy was the last thing on my mind as I struggled into my hotel bed at one in the morning. A few hours later, David Graveney and I were looking at the Folkestone wicket (reflecting on how it would play after Essex had reported one of the tracks there the previous game) when it suddenly dawned on me that I hadn't been told if I was captain or not. All the lads kept saying, 'Morning, captain' to me, so I assumed I was in charge. There was nobody there, apart from the players and scorer, to contradict me, so if they called me 'captain' that's what it would be! After all, I was senior professional, not vice-captain, but Proc clearly must have felt I'd realised I was to lead the side in his absence, so I went out and did the best thing – I won the toss. That was to prove an important event in a low-scoring game.

I thought the much-maligned Folkestone wicket a good one for

75

cricket. It was a long way from the infamous one used by Essex and it helped the spinners, while at the same time favouring a batsman who was prepared to chance his arm. Only one was – Zaheer – and he played a marvellous innings of 98. If ever a batsman deserved a century it was he. I went in at number 7 to try and calm him down, because he was playing like a millionaire. It didn't really work and I don't blame him for playing the wicket rather than its reputation. After all, he won us the game.

I enjoyed the tactical side of captaincy. When we batted, I fielded at slip and gully, although I soon moved out to mid-off when the ball started turning, and I made a point of bringing the spinners on early with the ball still hard, so they could grip it. I was very keen on democracy in the field, asking the opinions of everybody. I'm not saying that should always be the case, but I wanted to get all the lads involved and I think it worked; in a long season, you'll often see fielders walking around like zombies when the game is dying the death and I wanted our lads to be thinking, 'I'll have a word with Brainy about that idea.' Even Zaheer bucked up in the field; normally he walks around with his hands in his pockets down at third man and he sometimes strays about fifteen yards from where he should be, but in this match he was very switched on. This form of captaincy isn't meant as a criticism of Mike Procter, because he makes a point of asking the senior players for advice on the field, but I think county captains as a breed of men should be a little more demonstrative about taking all the team into their confidence.

Kent only needed 160-odd to win on the last day and for a while things went smoothly for us, with all the bowlers chipping in with wickets. Then we got into a bad spell, with Rowe and Asif holding us up. I came back on just before lunch and got Asif lbw. With my job done, I brought Graveney straight back to bowl at my end. Then Alan Knott started playing our spinners in his highly individualistic way. As he kept lapping them for boundaries with the aid of his superb eye and footwork, I suddenly thought, 'Oh Christ, we're going to lose this after being on top and I'll look a bloody fool.' After all, John Shepherd was still to come in. I thought I'd better come back on, because if anyone was going to lose the game, it might as well be me. As luck would have it, Alan Wilkins grabbed a wicket and I got Shepherd and Underwood in successive balls to win the game. It was all over within ten minutes of Wilkins and me coming back to bowl and I'd won my first game as a county captain. As I walked off the field, every one of our lads came up to me, shook my hand and congratulated me. A great moment.

The Kent lads were very good about their defeat. They almost seem resigned to the fact that they're on a bad trot, which is surprising considering the ability that's in their side. Imagine it – John Shepherd coming in number nine! Maybe one or two of their older players aren't so good any more but Alan Ealham's a good captain and a nice bloke. The crowds love him in Kent, and every time he picks up the ball in the field he gets a clap. Once in our game, he picked the ball up cleanly but sent a bad throw to the toes of Alan Knott behind the stumps, yet the crowd gave him a huge cheer. He was a tremendous fielder in the deep a few years back but now the demands of captaincy dictate that he fields nearer to the bat.

Only one thing marred my time in Folkestone. I had to report Zaheer to Tony Brown and Procter for refusing to attend a function in one of the sponsors' tents. I didn't want to do it, but I felt he'd undermined my authority by refusing to come with us. Luckily, all the others were happy to attend, but I don't know how I would have handled the situation if anybody else had followed Zaheer's lead, because I was put in the impossible position of asking the rest of the side to do something that one of the players had turned down. I made a point of discussing the whole thing openly in front of the team, so that there would be no question of a misunderstanding when it got back to Bristol. I told Zed that he only had to show his face for five minutes, have one quick drink, then he could leave. I knew that the sponsors wanted to see him and it wouldn't take that much time out of the night he planned to spend with Asif. The people who sponsor these games keep us in a living and if one of our team can't spend five minutes chatting in pleasant company, I despair. But Zed refused when I explained the situation to him, even when I told him I'd be reporting him to the club. He'd put my authority on the line, even if it was for just one game that I was in charge, and I had no other choice. When I told Procter and Brown about the incident, they said I had acted correctly. I have no idea what disciplinary action was subsequently taken.

On the way back home from Folkestone, I had plenty of time to discuss the Zaheer incident with my driving companions, not least of all because we were delayed for two hours in London due to a burst water main. My old team-mate, David Shepherd, had come down for the Kent match and his genial good nature was a godsend to us on that long journey. He also took the wheel through London, because I hate driving there. I've really missed 'Shep' since he retired last year. If you asked all county cricketers about him, you wouldn't find one bloke to say a bad word about him. He just lives for the game and he represents everything that is good about cricket – unselfish, good-humoured, sporting and a good batsman with an excellent temperament. Whenever he was dropped to make way for someone else, Shep was the first man to wish the new player all the luck in the world. Next season he hopes to be on the first-class umpires' list and he'll be very good at the job. He won't stand any nonsense, but he'll always be there with a cheery grin.

My travelling companions this summer have been more or less the same. David Partridge has been with me whenever he's been in the side; he's snoring so much this season, so perhaps he's getting used to the strains of county cricket. Andy Brassington has kept us all awake on those long journeys. He's the Derek Randall of our side, never still, always chattering and, it seems, never down-hearted. He loves to have an ice-cream and walk around the ground, starting up conversations with people he's never met. The day's never too long for Andy, he just loves everything about county cricket and he's a good advert for the game. Alan Wilkins has been with me on most journeys and he's settled in well in his first season with us. It's always difficult when you've come from another county, because you wonder if your new colleagues have heard some gossip from your previous club. I certainly felt that way for my first season after leaving Worcestershire. But Alan's a pleasant man who loves his crossword puzzles, and his arrival hasn't just helped the side in cricketing matters – he has a very beautiful wife and the sight of Mrs Wilkins does wonders for the team's morale! Completing my carload is Bert Avery, our scorer and general Mr Fixit. Bert organises our accommodation for away trips and loves the whole paraphernalia of county

78

cricket. The winters are always very long for Bert and he longs for the days when he can talk cricket over a pint and a fag with his Gloucestershire boys. A Gloucestershire man through and through, Bert gets very het up on occasions about the way we play, and he doesn't mince his words when we've played badly.

On that journey from Folkestone we travelled back in less style than our trip down, simply because I now had my Marina back. Lex Mead had sent down a bloke from Cheltenham in my car, so that at least I'd be able to get back up to Bristol after the game. He dropped the car off at Folkestone, caught a train up to where the Rover had been left and coaxed it back to Cheltenham. I thought that was tremendous of Lex, yet typical of him. After all, I'm one of the few county cricketers who can keep his sponsored car all the year round. Most of the pros have to hand them back within a month of the season's end.

So it was back to Bristol and the traditional Bank Holiday fixtures against Somerset, and what two great games we had with them. On the Sunday, Hallam Moseley hit the winning run off the last ball to win by one wicket, while the championship match was drawn in the most spectacular circumstances. But it wasn't just the cricket itself that was so intriguing. There was the Brian Rose story to digest for a start. Brian seemed to think he was going to play in the Centenary test within the next week, even though he'd been injured in the Leeds test a fortnight earlier. He could have played against us, but he decided not to risk it and get properly fit for the showpiece match at Lord's on the following Thursday. Rose was under the impression that some time in the nets was enough to guarantee his selection. So Ian Botham captained Somerset in Rose's absence and then, half an hour after the toss, Rose was told he wasn't in the England team. It all seemed a little beyond me, especially when Brian played for Somerset during the Centenary test. I felt desperately sorry for him, especially as he could have proved his fitness against us if his selection depended on that. I was impressed that he didn't run to the press and sell his story to the highest bidder.

The media were out in force for the Somerset match and their attentions were focused on one man – Ian Botham or, as one of the national papers had it, 'Bunter Botham'. There wasn't much news about, so Fleet Street seemed to have decided to go big on the Botham story. We were treated to all

79

sorts of articles about Botham's alleged weight problem during the Bank Holiday weekend, and it all got very boring. I thought it very sad that all they could comment on was the size of the England captain's stomach; nobody seemed interested in trying to analyse what had gone wrong with his bowling. It's not as if he's all that overweight – he's a big, wide-shouldered, large-boned lad who seems to get more muscular every time I see him, but he's not fat. Any clever cameraman or photographer can take shots of anybody at an unflattering angle so that they look fat – even me! Peter Denning showed what he thought of it all by fielding on the boundary with a sweater stuck up his shirt for a few overs, presumably in the hope that some daft cameraman might think he was Botham! Ian himself was superb in his dealings with the media. At lunch on the Monday he shouted to some of the cameramen, 'Hey, do you want to come and see what I'm eating? It's steak and salad!' and every time any of the crowd jeered him, he'd wave back at them. All of a sudden, the media lost interest and the cameras were taken down.

I felt sorry for him, especially in the evening when he kept himself to himself with Viv Richards and didn't do what he normally does – have a few pints and a chat with the players. He obviously felt that if he was seen having a pint, a flash bulb would appear from somewhere. I also felt sorry for him on the field because he was clearly not fit. He looked just an arm bowler, and he wasn't putting his back into his delivery at all. He bowled mediocre medium pace, which was inadvisable. Ian's the sort of bloke who has to prove himself to the public, and I felt sad that he didn't resist the temptation to forget about bowling again till he was fully fit. He's unbalanced the test side all summer because he's not really fit to bowl; because of his inconsistency as a batsman, he has to be judged as an all-rounder in a Test team, so that if he's not fit to bowl, he shouldn't be playing. I'm worried that Ian might find it increasingly hard to sustain the amazing standards he's set himself, in which case he might get dispirited and give it all up soon. He's made enough cash already to get out of the game.

England were on a hiding to nothing in the West Indies series and there's no point in blaming Botham too much for our poor showing. The selectors knew he was learning his trade, so did the public and press – and if it hadn't been for prolonged rain, we would have lost by a heavier margin. We lost our best chance at Trent Bridge, when Bob Willis so nearly won the game with his own great efforts. But, as I suspected at the time, it took a lot out of him. I was sorry to see Mike Hendrick and Bob Woolmer fail to do themselves justice; Hendrick never really looked fit and perhaps he was brought back too soon, while Woolmer fell away after a good start to the season. He hadn't played test cricket for three years and he seemed just a little out of touch as a result. For all that, he looked fairly safe and perhaps he deserved more than two tests to get used to the pressures again. Alan Knott also disappointed: his ability behind the stumps was still there but his batting fell away terribly. It looked as if he was shell-shocked from two years of dodging bouncers in World Series Cricket. At the start of the series, I thought Knott, Hendrick and Woolmer were crucial men in England's strategy, but they all failed. Botham can't be blamed for that.

Botham's critics forget how much effort he's put into his job. Before he ever got in the England team, he'd bowl and bowl for Somerset, have a few beers at night, then bat and bowl again the next day. But since 1977 he's been a round-the-year cricketer, working his heart out for England. He's carried England and there's only so much even a fantastically strong lad like Ian can achieve. In a few years time we'll sit back and say what a great player Ian Botham was, so why can't people enjoy him now, forget about his weight problem, keep their fingers crossed that his back complaint clears up and stop writing him off just because he hasn't yet proved to be a great captain? He's such an exciting cricketer, of a type foreign to England; he's box-office, there's an aura about him and I just hope he doesn't burn himself out, because we need cricketers like him.

The same applies to his close friend, Viv Richards. I always thought Peter May was the best batsman I'd ever bowled against, but perhaps that was youthful hero-worship clouding my judgement. One shot Viv played against me on the Monday morning of this match changed my mind. He'd come in on Saturday night and played some good shots as I followed my theory that the best way to bowl at him was to bounce him out. I bowled too short and not quick enough and I was easy meat to him. I bowled much better on Monday morning and my

81

confidence was growing until I bowled him a ball of good length and reasonable pace. It was the kind of ball that Mike Hendrick specialises in: a normal batsman couldn't drive it and it wasn't short enough to cut. Anyway, Viv went forward, waited for it, then smashed it straight into the ground and it went like a rocket between me and mid-off. It was the finest shot ever played against me and I applauded him. Among modern batsmen, I think only Procter could play a shot like that against such a good length ball.

It's a great contest, matching one's own professionalism against the genius of Viv. He's all out to psych you when he's at the crease: he looks arrogant and effortless and glares at you to let you know he's in charge. He seems to be saying, 'You bowl where you like, I'll hit you where I like' and I've seen people frightened to bowl at him because they've been mentally dominated by him. That doesn't work with me. In this innings, he hit me for two fours in a row, the first an off-drive and the second a hook which landed twenty yards in front of square and clattered to the boundary. He just stood there, tapping the bat handle with his palm, and stared at me. The next ball came straight back at me, I picked it up and went to throw it back at his stumps, in case he was out of his ground. I didn't but he put his hand up and smiled back at me. From then on it was a good day, and Viv chatted away to me whenever he was the non-striker – which wasn't very often!

The only thing to do with Viv is to bowl line and length and keep your chin up. If you bowl him a good length ball outside off stump and he whips you through mid-wicket for a four, grit your teeth and keep trying. If it's his day, console yourself with the thought that the crowd are enjoying it. And whatever you do, don't drop him. We did that when he'd scored 70 and I remember saying to one of our lads, 'Next time he gives a chance he'll be on 170.' Prophetic words – an hour or so later, I happened to glance at the scoreboard as David Graveney ran in to bowl and noticed that Viv was on 171. Viv sliced that ball to me at backward point and I caught him low down. It's a weird game sometimes.

Somerset got fourteen points from this match and we picked up eight, even though the game ended with the scores level. It doesn't seem fair, really: they got the extra points because they batted second in a match where the scores were level at the end, but we contributed in equal part to a great finish. They needed 201 in thirty-eight overs and for a time they were skating home. But then Viv was out first ball for nought – he'd been suffering from a virus and took an eternity to walk out to the crease, so perhaps his 170 had taken it out of him the day before.

Anyway, I had to bowl the last over with Somerset needing six to win with four wickets in hand. I hadn't bowled for some time and I was very stiff, but I told myself I just had to get through those six balls. In the event they scored two runs off my first two deliveries, then I bowled Nigel Popplewell third ball. Colin Dredge and Peter Roebuck scrambled three off the next two deliveries, so they needed just one to win off the last ball, with Roebuck on strike. Proc asked me, 'What are you going to bowl?' and I said, 'As fast and as straight as I can.' He agreed. We got Andy Brassington to stand up to the stumps to prevent them running a quick single to the keeper and I ran in to bowl. It was just the delivery I'd prayed for – a yard quicker than the others and just over the middle stump. Brassy shouted out, 'Well bowled' and that's when all hell broke loose. Roebuck had realised that the bails were still on at my end and shouted 'Run!' to Dredge. I was walking down to Roebuck's end, chuffed to bits with myself, and I didn't know what to make of the sight of Roebuck tearing past me, closely pursued by our keeper! All Brassy had to do was throw the ball to Graveney at the bowler's end but he went for the dive with Roebuck. They both launched themselves at the crease and ended up neck and neck. God knows who got there first but luckily, umpire Ken Palmer had the presence of mind to call 'time' as they dived for the crease. If Somerset had won because of that, all hell would have broken loose. Proc would have been up in their dressing room sharpish, because he was mad at Roebuck. He shouted, 'If that's the way you want to play the game, take the bloody points then,' to which Roebuck quietly answered, 'I like to win.' I think Roebuck was right and I wonder how many cricketers would have had his presence of mind in a tight finish to realise that there was still a chance of a run. All Andy Brassington had to do was pull a stump out at his end and the game would have been over but he got caught up in the heat of the moment.

Even if it wasn't fair that they got more points than us, cricket was the winner in both this match and the Sunday one where we really made them fight after batting badly. Proc was injured and I captained the side in the field and really enjoyed it. I always enjoy the games against Somerset because there's atmosphere and they have a lot of players who love to attack. One player in their team who never gets many headlines is Colin Dredge, their tall seamer. Now I really rate this bloke: he's tall, hits the deck and the splice of the bat. He hardly ever bowls a half-volley, a complete contrast to Botham. He reminds me a little of Lancashire's Peter Lee and if there was one bloke in the country I could have in our side as third seamer it would be him. He can bat a bit too, he plays straight and can hold you up.

Despite that setback at Bristol we were still in good heart, and we then proceeded to outplay Warwickshire at Edgbaston. We were 272 in front with six wickets in hand but rain washed out the whole of the last day's play. I know a lot of our lads felt we wouldn't have bowled them out twice on a flat Edgbaston wicket, but the Warwickshire batsmen were low in confidence at the time and I fancied our chances. If we'd managed a win we would have gone to third position in the table, but that would have been a false position, I feel. Still, we showed our strengths in this match: Chris Broad played and missed a lot but grafted well for his century, Sadiq looked good in the second innings and I was very pleased with my long spell on the second morning. Because it was a flat wicket I just ran in and bowled as quickly as I could, and I made a few of them hop around a bit, as well as catching David Smith a painful blow on the elbow. I was again impressed by Smith; despite his injury he battled away, got in line and made a good fifty.

Apart from Dilip Doshi, who bowled beautifully in both innings, the Warwickshire players looked low and tired. They were due to play their vital John Player League match on the following Sunday against Leicester and I sensed a sort of quiet desperation creeping in, a feeling that they'd come so far only to be thwarted at the finishing post. Bob Willis didn't look fully fit, although he bowled very well off a short run-up; he's a positive leader and he's got the team behind him, but even he's beginning to feel the pressure. He turned round and gave some hecklers a real mouthful when he misfielded the ball and although there's no real excuse for that, I could sympathise with Bob. Just because people have paid their money, that doesn't give them the freedom to indulge in personal abuse. I probably would have done the same thing as Bob and regretted it instantly.

Steve Rouse, their experienced seam bowler, was terribly down when I had a drink with him on the first evening; he hadn't been bowling all that well recently and his head was crammed with all sorts of theories. He'd even been told to hold the ball differently – after all these years of professional cricket! David Brown has helped him, and so he should with all his bowling experience, but Dennis Amiss has confused him with some theories and I told Dennis so after I'd watched Steve bowl. I don't think a batsman is a good judge of what a bowler's doing wrong, whereas a fellow-bowler knows what to look for. Steve asked me to have a look at him in the nets the following day and I watched him from all angles. He's the kind of guy who bowls through his action, rather than putting any great body movement into it, and I suggested a couple of amendments. I also told him to put out of his head all that nonsense about changing his grip on the ball – I'll always remember Max Walker's words to me on the last Australian tour when he told me that he simply rotated his grip on the ball till he found one that helped him move the ball off the wicket. Max used to ask Rodney Marsh if the ball was hitting the seam and he'd alter his grip until he managed that consistently. He wasn't one for too much technical mumbo-jumbo and his record wasn't bad, either. I was sorry that dear old 'Tiger' Smith wasn't there to advise Steve Rouse; 'Tiger' was a fount of cricket knowledge and he passed many a good tip on to me as he sat watching the cricket till well into his nineties. But he'd been dead a year by this time and Steve didn't quite know what to do. I told him all he needed was five wickets in an innings to boost his confidence and after that it would all come right. It's really a simple game after all.

We left Edgbaston and its vast empty stadium and headed through the rain for a more relaxed atmosphere – Devon. Gloucestershire had to play a game for the centenary celebrations of Tavistock Cricket Club and it was nice to meet up with some friendly old faces from the past. Mine host at the local pub is none other than my old mate, Jack Davey, who played for us until 1978. Jack was a good seamer in his time and he's invested his benefit money shrewdly in a pub. He still plays a bit of cricket for Tavistock and it was nice to see a bloke who'd put a lot into county cricket in a good frame of mind, enjoying his new career.

We have a good relationship with the Tavistock club, who have helped our beneficiaries out a lot over the years, and it was a pleasure to play down there that weekend. It was hard going, though, for our three overseas players. Naturally they had to turn up at the match to boost the gate but they'd already contracted to play in a double-wicket competition at Scarborough. Fortunately, Zaheer and Sadiq were knocked out of the competition on the Saturday, so they could travel down to Tavistock on the Sunday morning, following an overnight stop in Birmingham. But poor old Procter suffered once more from his own competitiveness and all-round skill. He had reached the final at Scarborough, scheduled for the Monday, so he had to travel down to Tavistock on the Sunday morning, bat in the match and then get back into his car and travel another 370 miles to Scarborough in the afternoon! He was as good as gold about it and luckily for his peace of mind, he won the Scarborough competition and a few bob into the bargain. I think he deserved it.

Jack Davey's success in his new career started off again in my mind the old doubts about my financial insecurity. As Jack happily told me about the trip to Tenerife he was due to take with his family, all the old worries came flooding back. 'You lucky old devil, Jack,' I thought. 'When could I afford to take the Brain family of five to Tenerife?' Of course, I didn't begrudge my mate a penny of his lot, but I realised how lucky he'd been to stay at one county during his career, thereby qualifying for a benefit that proved to be a good one. With that financial security, his business horizons had broadened and he seemed set up for life in his flourishing pub. I'd shelved thoughts of retirement for the last few weeks; the team had suddenly clicked so that it had again become a pleasure to play cricket, and the great thrill of captaining Gloucestershire successfully had kept me going on elation for quite a time. But, as I drove back home from Devon on that first glorious day of September, I resolved to get things sorted out that week.

The club either read my mind or it was simply a quirk of fate – but the next day, I was told that I was getting a testimonial. I must emphasise here and now that at no stage did I put a pistol to anyone's head at Gloucestershire County Cricket Club. I never threatened to pack it all in if things didn't go my way and I never assumed I would be awarded a testimonial so soon after being capped in 1977. Of course I had some hopes, and Mike Procter has always said I deserve something from my time in cricket – and for that matter the chairman, Ken Graveney, had been very optimistic in my talks with him in the last few weeks – but I never dared build up my hopes, only to have them dashed. When you've been capped in 1966 by Worcestershire and then get the sack the year before you're due to qualify for a benefit, you tend to look on the pessimistic side. So all this came out of the blue on that Tuesday afternoon and I hardly took any notice of the words from the cricket committee chairman, Don Stone, that my testimonial was actually due to start on 1 October, and that I'd better pull my finger out. As I was collecting my thoughts Sadiq came out of Tony Brown's office, told me he'd been awarded a benefit in 1982, shook my hand and wished me all the luck in the world. I appreciated that – after all, he'd been capped in 1973 and was ahead of me in the queue, but he was delighted that his turn would come after me.

The Brain carload that rattled down to Brighton that afternoon for our next match was a pretty happy collection. Everybody was very good about it and I'd like to think their congratulations were sincere. I couldn't begin to tell them what it meant to me. Until that afternoon I'd lived with insecurity since my debut in county cricket in 1959. I'd simply lived from day to day, dreading the time when my bowling would suddenly go down the pan. I was never able to put the bad days in perspective, I'd always worry about walking out of cricket with nothing to show for it. I can't live on the past, I have to be judged on my last performance and that's one of the main reasons why I occasionally seem negative. It's all very well being told that you're a good bowler, but you need something to aim for, to help ease the pain of bowing out of a great way of life. I've got that security now and I'll do everything I can to repay my gratitude to Gloucestershire. They gave me back my self-respect in 1976 when I was wondering if I was too old to play county cricket and thinking about running a pub, and now they give me a testimonial after such a short time with them. Tremendous.

87

I had another reason to be happy on Tuesday 2 September. I was skipper again. Proc had to attend a registration meeting at Lord's for the committee to consider whether he was qualified for selection for England, so I was in charge. Obviously it wasn't as big a thrill as the Folkestone match, not least because we were on the end of a hammering. I lost the toss and we were a long way behind Sussex when the rain washed out the final day. Zaheer was out injured and, with Procter not playing, we had a very young batting side that didn't acquit itself well against the pace of Imran Khan. Sussex are a good, sound side; Mendis looks better every time I see him and Colin Wells is an extremely confident young batsman. He gives the bowler the full face of the bat, plays the good balls sensibly and hammers the bad ones with a Botham-like flourish. He reached his 1,000 runs for the championship season in this match and I was very impressed with him.

I wasn't too impressed by two of our young lads when I offered the number three batting place to them. As we were so short of batting experience, I asked Sadiq to bat lower down at number four to give us solidity. He readily agreed and I asked David Partridge and then Martin Stovold to go in first wicket down. Now both lads were worried about their form and they also hadn't played even a second XI match for a couple of weeks, but I firmly believe you've got to grab every opportunity you can to bat high up in the hundred-over limit game. I told them that I understood the situation but that I was disappointed. Times have changed and I don't want to sound an old fogey, but if a few years ago a young player had refused to bat where he was asked by his captain, he wouldn't have played again. In the end I asked Phil Bainbridge, a man out of form, to bat number three and he said promptly, 'Yes, please.' He failed, but he showed character and gave it a go.

So to the last game of the season, a time all cricket-lovers not actively involved in playing county cricket dread. I can understand the frustration of a lovely warm September with little county cricket to watch but believe me, the professionals are just about all in by the start of August and many of us are just hanging on for the season's end. It's not that we don't like playing the game, more that it's so difficult for captains to fire the enthusiasm of their players in the last few weeks when there's little to play for. I think we've done well to keep going at

Gloucestershire, considering that our season ended, in trophy terms, in mid-July when we were knocked out of the Gillette Cup. Ours is still a happy dressing room and I don't really see much evidence of people getting on each other's nerves after four months of being in close proximity.

We didn't really end the season on a high note – a thrashing in the John Player League at the hands of Derbyshire. Andy Stovold was the only man to get any runs and they strolled home by six wickets. Geoff Miller batted well for them, steadying everything down and looking, as usual, a well-coached, orthodox batsman who knows his own limitations. He's a good captain, too, and Derbyshire are a well-knit unit. They've got some high quality players, particularly Peter Kirsten. Proc had told me about him a few years back, when he said the best three young South African batsmen were Wessels, Lamb and Kirsten, and he was absolutely right about them. Kirsten's foot-work is superb. He gets down the wicket to the seam bowlers as well as the spinners and anybody who scores three unbeaten double hundreds in a wet English season has got class. John Wright is a fine, sound opening batsman, Barry Wood has still a lot of shrewdness to offer, Steve Oldham will be an even better seamer next year and all in all, I fancy Derbyshire to win something next season.

So, nearly six months after I had my first bowl of the decade in the Bristol nets, and 12,000 miles later, it was all over for another year. Or was it? There was still the trip to Barbados in a few days time, one of the many advantages of my re-think about retiring. A lot of our lads will spend the winter coaching or playing abroad after the Barbados tour, a salutary reminder to me of how the game's changed in my time. In the old days, the last match of the season would end with some of us saying, 'See you at skittles down the local next week.' Now the modern cricketer's closing remark is often, 'Can you give me a lift to the airport next week?' Certainly it's a far cry from the days when I joined many of my fellow-pros in the autumnal rush to sign on the dole.

Barbados

On Saturday 13 September we flew out to Barbados for our short tour. For me it was a chance to top the 100,000 miles mark in flights abroad to play cricket; despite my comparative anonymity as a pro cricketer, I've been lucky enough to play in places like Malawi, Honolulu and the United States with my two counties, and I relished the chance to see the small Caribbean island that's fostered so many great players.

It's a beautiful place and interest in the game is fanatical out there. The temperature was in the nineties every day of our fortnight stay, the beaches were as white and the sea as blue as any travel brochure indicates. It's almost impossible to believe that this tiny island, measuring just twenty-seven miles long and fourteen miles wide, is so important to the well-being of West Indies cricket. Yet their Test players are treated like gods over there; Joel Garner came to see us in one match, and the eyes of the kids never left him from the moment he got out of his car till he walked into the pavilion. The standard of club cricket is very good indeed and the wickets are reasonable, but one thing I just couldn't get over was the size of the Kennington Oval, where England will be playing a Test in a few months time. It's minute, smaller than Taunton. Michael Holding will be starting his run-up from the boundary's edge, and the ground will be absolutely bursting to the seams if they get 15,000 people in there. The dressing rooms are about the size of a normal living room and there's just one shower – in a Test Match ground! Ian Botham will love that, it'll remind him of the Taunton facilities.

Twelve players went on the trip, plus Tony Brown and our coach, Graham Wiltshire, backed up by thirty of our members. A guest player for us was Peter Roebuck of Somerset and he captained us in one of our games. We played five matches, winning three of them, and the competition was fairly fierce. In the game against the Wanderers Club I bowled at Tony Cozier, the well-known radio commentator. My fourth ball he gloved to Andy Stovold for the biggest dolly catch you've ever seen, yet he stood there and waited to be given out! Professionalism from an amateur, I suppose.

I bumped into Desmond Haynes when we played his club, Carlton, and he greeted me like a long-lost brother. That was strange, because when we played the West Indians at Bristol in July, Desmond hardly said a word to us, but this time he was perfectly charming. He took us to a rum shop which was owned by his mother and we had a marvellous time. The prices weren't bad, either – a bottle of rum and six Cokes cost me just over £2!

We met up with Clyde Walcott and his brother, Keith, and I was interested to hear some of the locals say that Keith might have been an even greater player than Clyde given enough good fortune. I had a fascinating chat over dinner with that fine batsman of the sixties, Seymour Nurse, and I wished some of our young batsmen had been there with me to hear the words of wisdom. Seymour bemoaned the fact that too many youngsters don't watch the cricket from the dressing room before they go into bat. They get bored easily and find other ways to occupy their time, yet there's so much to be learned from watching and listening. One example from Seymour hammered home the point: the West Indians were playing Essex and he was next man in at number four. The number five batsman was fidgeting away and Seymour told him, 'For God's sake sit down and watch the cricket, you might learn something.' But he didn't and Seymour went in, then was dismissed cheaply. In walks the next man, only to be run out halfway on the second run to Robin Hobbs at third man. He comes out and says, 'That bloke can throw a bit, can't he?' Grunts Seymour, 'If you'd only sat and watched him field earlier, you'd still be at the wicket.' Seymour's philosophy was that if you can find an extra run from somewhere, or find out who are the great fielders from watching a whole day's play, then you should have your eyes glued on the cricket. Quite right, too.

All the talk on our trip was about the England tour in the New Year and I couldn't help feeling worried for our lads because there's a lot of anti-white feeling being stirred up out there. I think Roland Butcher's time isn't going to be all that pleasant because many Barbadians feel he's been disloyal by opting to play for England. It'll be a real test of character for Butcher and for the whole England team. I'd love to see a Test at the Oval in Barbados, but from the safety of the pavilion, not among the crowd. The England players will face a hard time from the spectators, and the taunts and jeers won't be just about their cricket abilities. Anyone who fields out on the boundary's edge will deserve sympathy and God help them if they actually win a Test. There could be a riot. Everything's being whipped up into a fervour and the fact that England managed luckily to avoid a thrashing in the recent series has only doubled the intensity of feeling. Tony Cozier told me that the only reason why Andy Roberts wasn't going to Pakistan with the West Indian team was to get him fit and ready for the English batsmen – as if he needs any incentive.

I'm genuinely worried for our lads, because although a few of them have been out there on little jaunts, most of them haven't experienced the unique test match atmosphere. It's going to be bad enough in a comparatively friendly place like Barbados, but in Jamaica and Guyana the anti-English feeling will be worse. That may well help to bind the England boys together, but no matter how tight a unit they are off the field, some of them could struggle under the pressure of a test in that atmosphere. Some will thrive on it – Botham for a start. They'll love him out there because he plays their kind of way and he'll turn round and give them a few signs whenever he feels like it. Boycott will go his own sweet way in his quest to become the greatest test run-maker of all time and his temperament is so good that he'll shut the noise right out of his consciousness. I can see combative characters like Gatting and Bairstow also enjoying the occasion but they're really going to earn their money.

I'm very concerned for our fast bowlers. It's all very well saying that the heat makes you looser and helps you bowl quicker but it can sap your strength as well. Old and Willis don't exactly blossom in the heat and I hope they stick Willis on the beach and just play him in the tests, because they'll really need his bounce. I don't think Dilley was all that great a selection, because he might be suspect after his bout of glandular fever and apart from that, he lacks experience of bowling long spells – a casualty of the modern, hundred-over limit game if ever there was one. I can see Botham and Stevenson doing a lot of donkey work. I hope Botham's super-fit by the New Year because he's going to have to perform like a superman. Stevenson is strong and willing, with a Yorkshireman's commitment to the cause, and I think he'll end up a big success out there. Despite the racial undertones, I think Butcher's selection a good one. Last season Ray Illingworth told me he would have taken Butcher to Australia, because he takes the bowlers on. He's got a magnificent eye and if everything clicks one day, he could win a test in a couple of hours. Those boundaries are very short indeed out there and Butcher and Gooch might just be the men to capitalise on that.

But the small boundaries also mean there'll be a great responsibility on our spinners to bowl tightly. Tall spin bowlers who can bounce the ball are needed on those wickets and that's why the selection of Emburey, and not Underwood, is sound. But Willey and Miller aren't high-class support bowlers and a lot will depend on Emburey. The same applies to David Gower, a man lucky to be selected in my opinion. Nobody admires his talent more than I do, but he hasn't made enough runs in county cricket to justify his recall to the England team. How can Bill Athey be good enough for the Centenary test against Australia at the end of August, yet not be good enough for the West Indies tour party when it was announced a fortnight later? It doesn't make sense to me.

Downton could prove to be a good investment for the future. He's a neat, unhurried keeper and I was impressed by his batting this summer. He doesn't hit the ball very far, but he'll nudge and work the ball away. I'm just not sure about his temperament. He's a nice, quiet lad who might just shrivel up in that hothouse. I'd dearly love to see men like Ken Barrington, John Edrich and Basil D'Oliveira walking out to bat for England on the West Indian tour. They weren't the prettiest batsmen ever to play for us, but they were test match players in every other way – guts, temperament, concentration and the desire to score big hundreds. At the moment, I can see only Boycott possessing those credentials.

I really want Ian Botham to ram all the recent criticism down countless throats. If ever a tour party needed inspiration from its captain, it's this one. I can't remember a young, untried captain who faced a trickier year than Botham – a

93

home and away series against the world champions, plus a home series against Australia next summer. I just pray he shakes off the surprisingly negative attitude he's shown so far as skipper. That Centenary test was very disappointing from a cricket point of view, apart from all the other hassles. I believe Botham should have made more of an effort to go for the runs on that last day. It was a very fair declaration, the Aussies were one bowler short and after all, it was a one-off occasion. The Ashes weren't at stake, the ground was chock-full of real enthusiasts, thirsting for a few memories to warm them through the winter months, but England played it tightly and didn't risk defeat. The Gloucestershire team watched the afternoon session in a TV lounge in our hotel at Hove and with an hour to go, we were so disappointed at England's tactics that we all walked out. Botham didn't lead from the front in that game and he should realise that if he captains the side in the same way as he plays cricket, he'll make a lot of friends. If you lose a test ot two, so what? I think we'll lose heavily in the West Indies, but I hope we go down with a flourish rather than just attempt to hang on for five days.

Looking at the prospects for the tour, all I can say is 'Thank God I'm forty!' because I wouldn't fancy it at all. For the first time, I shan't be wishing I was an England player when they fly out.

Autumn Reflections

As I watch my Barbadian sun-tan fade and see the last of the duty-free rum slip down my friends' throats at home in Worcester, I find myself reflecting on the 1980 season and feeling depressed. Financially, I had the marvellous news about my testimonial but in broader terms it wasn't a great season for cricket. Too many unsavoury things spoiled its image – slow over-rates, increasing misbehaviour by the players, a poor, unimaginative England team and those dreadful crowd scenes at the Centenary test – and the weather was appalling, the worst in all my time in the game.

Gloucestershire were erratic, fluctuating between irresistible form and maddening defeats that were often self-inflicted. We must have been marvellous value to watch, judging by all the close finishes we had in every competition, but we lacked consistency, that quality which wins trophies. All our staff have been re-engaged for next season and I suspect our improved showing in the championship in the last month had a lot to do with that. We finished seventh in the table, compared to last year's tenth, and we were just seven points behind Sussex, the fourth team. But anything higher would have been flattering, despite the way we stormed through after entering August without a single win. I won't be terribly popular in some circles for stating this but our batting let us down all summer; only Lancashire, Kent and Hampshire got less batting points than our thirty-nine, and they all finished in the bottom three. If our batsmen had done their job properly we would have finished in the top three, and I get sick and tired of people describing us as a strong batting side. Bonus points are usually won by the first six batsmen and three of our first five are world-class players. Not one of them averaged over forty, and compare that with overseas batsmen for other counties. In the top eleven of the national batting averages, seven overseas players averaged over fifty. None of them played for Gloucestershire. Zaheer got out too often when well set, Sadiq lost his touch for long periods and didn't get one hundred, while Procter only came good in August, when he made nearly 600 of his 1,081 runs.

We're supposed to be a poor bowling side, yet five of us were around the fifty-wicket mark and only Middlesex, the champions, got more bowling points than our seventy-four: That was the same figure as Surrey, who finished second, with Robin Jackman and Sylvester Clarke knocking over batsmen regularly. Middlesex – with men like van der Bijl, Daniel, Selvey, Emburey, Titmus and Edmonds – only got six points more than us. We found a bowler in Alan Wilkins, who just needs a little more confidence to improve even further, our two spin bowlers continued to improve, Procter finished in the national top ten despite injury problems and B. M. Brain didn't do all that badly either. In fact I got exactly the same amount of wickets this season in the championship and John Player League as in 1979 – seventy-three to be precise. Considering that I was bowling in twelve-over spells as a strike bowler, I'm quite pleased with my 1980 season, despite niggling little injuries.

In the John Player League we had some great finishes but you expect to win or lose games by a couple of runs. Nevertheless, two more victories would have put us joint fourth rather than tenth.

I honestly feel that in a couple of years Gloucestershire will have a good side. Not many folk realise that the England Under-19 squad contains five boys from our county who are not yet on the staff. Lads like Broad, Wilkins, Brassington, Martin Stovold and Windaybank will get better. I'm not so sure about David Partridge and Phil Bainbridge, two players I've had great hopes for in recent years. David's an enigma. He seems to get fixations in his head about batting or bowling and he simply doesn't do himself justice. I think he's a little immature and I just don't know how we can get the best out of his obvious talent as an all-rounder. It's a tragedy for me to see someone like Phil Bainbridge struggle with the bat all season; his batting went back as his bowling improved and by the end of the summer he was a number 8 batsman and third seamer – and that doesn't seem right to me.

Andy Brassington had a fine season behind the stumps,

finishing second in the victims list behind Surrey's Jack Richards. I'd put him in the top five keepers in the country (along with Alan Knott, Derbyshire's Bob Taylor, Paul Downton of Middlesex and Jack Richards) but I think it was right not to send him to the West Indies with the England squad. Andy must work at his batting if he's going to win any caps; Downton has done just that, and he's not any better behind the stumps. Until then, Andy will keep trying his hardest and enjoying life. If he can only settle down a little behind the sticks, eliminate some of the dives in favour of anticipation, he'll get even better.

I was pleased to see John Childs get wickets towards the end of the season. A mediocre bat and fielder, John's that rarity in the modern game: a specialist bowler. He has a lovely action, bags of talent and a very good striking rate. Left-arm spinners tend to improve with age and I think John will be no different. I'm worried about Alastair Hignell, though. After a fine start to the season he went back a little. Injuries didn't help, but I think he also got a few theories crammed into his head. He has such a magnificent sportsman's eye that I feel he should hit everything in his arc and forget about the finesse. He has the gift of timing and power of stroke, yet to me he's gone back a little.

Another player who didn't do himself justice was Andy Stovold. A natural stroke-maker, he missed out on his thousand runs and didn't get a hundred. Andy's always theorising about wickets and what he should eat and drink; he goes through phases when he won't eat any potatoes, yet consumes lots of sweet things to give himself energy. He'll drink only pineapple juice and soda, then get fed up with that and have a few pints of lager. Anybody who saw him play that marvellous knock in the 1977 Benson and Hedges Cup Final knows about Andy Stovold's class and I hope his decline is only temporary.

The fact that the greatest innings and the best piece of bowling I saw from any side this season were both the work of one man, shows what a fine performer our captain still is. But Mike Procter has played a lot of cricket now over a long period of time and we musn't think he'll be able to keep pulling it out of the hat for us. His figures with both bat and ball declined from 1979 and our supporters will have to get used to seeing

Proc bowl less and less off his long run. As Worcestershire will testify, he can still swing the ball devastatingly, but even a strong body like Mike's can only take so much punishment over the years. I think we'll see him bowling his off-spinners for a long time to come because he hates to be idle, but I'd dearly love to see him acquire real consistency with his batting. On his day there are few finer sights than the majestic Procter and very few bowlers get him out – he does the work for them.

Perhaps Mike's successor as seam bowler will be David Surridge. Unfortunately we had no real chance to assess David's quality because he broke down early on with back trouble. He suffered from inflammation of the disc, possibly caused by bowling off a shortened run and trying to put too much whippiness into his delivery. He'd never played John Player League cricket before so he wasn't used to a short run-up. He's basically a rhythm bowler who needs a longer run to bowl quickly. I was terribly sorry for him and I know how he felt. When I came to Bristol, desperate to prove a lot of people wrong, I did my groin early on in the 1976 season and I fretted for quite a time. David was very keen to impress in his debut season with us and perhaps he tried too hard. He's a nice, intelligent lad who wants to know all the ins and outs of his injury. He won't know the extent of it for a few more months and we're all keeping our fingers crossed for him. He looked lively in those first few weeks and in view of his record – good, cheap wickets in 1979 with Cambridge University and a successful tour of Australia with Combined Universities – I think he would be a distinct asset to Gloucestershire.

I don't know who will succeed Mike as Gloucestershire captain, nor do I know when that will happen. He's with us for at least a couple more years and although he captained us much better last season compared with 1979, I know he'd like to hand over to someone else after another year. It won't be me – I've had my moment of glory and I'm too old anyway. I hope his successor is David Graveney. He's a very deep thinker, a man worth his place in the team on ability, and I suspect the extra responsibility would improve his game even further. One of the great wicket-prodders of our times, he'll go out about six times before play starts, mutter to himself knowledgeably, phone up for a local weather report – and he'll still get his forecast wrong about the way the wicket will play! But I think that he would be good for the county that's always been associated with the Graveney name, and in terms of cricket ability, character and temperament, there'd be no need at all for anyone to suggest favouritism. I think he would simply be the best man for the job, and to hell with the cynics.

But for the moment, issues like the captaincy, our batting and next season's NatWest Trophy tie in Ireland (we always do well on overseas tours!) are all taking a back seat as I throw myself into my testimonial work. It is for my services to cricket, not just for my five seasons with Gloucestershire, although the award is up to the individual club and is given to popular or deserving players, not just indiscriminately. It runs from 1 October 1980 to 30 September 1981, and the ramifications would tax the brain of a Denis Healey. The Cricketers' Association and the TCCB called all those having benefits or testimonials to a meeting at Edgbaston and the list of do's and don'ts was spelled out in great detail. I have to appoint a committee and the money raised will, I hope, express the gratitude of many who enjoy watching cricket. I shall be very reliant on bat raffles, golf tournaments, race evenings and dances. Gloucestershire will also make a donation. I'll certainly work hard enough for the cash and I'm looking forward to the busiest winter of my life. I just hope my form doesn't suffer next season, because I haven't known many beneficiaries who had good seasons on the field. But paradoxically, I should do better now that my nagging insecurities have been eased.

I might even get a contribution from that famous punk group, Brian Brain. I finally caught up with their band of alleged music after the season ended – and a working knowledge of the laws of libel forbids me to comment in great detail. Suffice it to say that there's no danger that illustrious tracks like 'Dirty Dealing in the Lone Star State', 'Jet Boats Up the Ganges', 'The Hots for You', and 'I've Got Pain' are likely to displace singers like Barry White, Suzi Quatro and Johnny Mathis on the Brain car cassette. The Brian Brain LP called 'Unexpected Noises' surely wins the award for the Most Apt Title of the Year, and I see from the sleeve notes that their fans can get a free Brian Brain poster from a certain address. I wonder if it's of a group of pink-haired youngsters or of an ageing seam bowler in cricket whites?

I expect to get quite a lot of comments this winter from

cricket lovers about the state of our game. Quite honestly, I share the sense of foreboding many have about the standards of county cricket. The abilities of individual players are the worst I've known in my time in cricket and it grieves me to say that. The best bowlers and batsmen are either too old or foreign and despite the way the game has changed, I don't think that ability belonging to another era would necessarily wither if it was tested today. That Worcestershire side of 1965 was the finest I've played in and it's nonsense to say that men like Graveney, Kenyon, Horton, Headley, Flavell, Coldwell, Booth and D'Oliveira would have struggled in the modern, all-action game. They would just have trained harder and their natural talent would have seen them through. There's now too much concentration on fitness to the detriment of individual skill. Men like Les Jackson, Tony Brown, Alan Moss, Jack Flavell, Derek Shackleton and Don Bates were far better bowlers than most of today's crop, and where are the English batsmen to compare with the late 'fifties collection of May, Cowdrey, Dexter, Graveney, Barrington, Smith and Edrich? I know what breed of English batsmen I'd rather bowl at.

But I'm even more worried about behaviour on the field. Now I'm no angel when it comes to a curse or two, but I've always been well aware of the code of conduct and I've never cheated in my life. Yet I didn't see one batsman walk in the 1980 season. They stand there, look at the bat if it's an lbw, and take an eternity to drag themselves from the crease, all the while looking back at the umpire. And the fielding side is no better – all this 'catch it' stuff when the ball's come off the pad isn't just a product of tension, it's often sheer gamesmanship. This year I've seen people who have blatantly gloved it to the keeper still standing there, waiting to be given out, and that's diabolical. When I started in county cricket, the ones who didn't walk could be counted on the fingers of one hand and they'd be given a huge rocket from their captains if they stood their ground when they knew they were out. I remember the time I walked when I wasn't out – in 1969 when Glamorgan only needed to beat us to win the county championship. I was batting with Vanburn Holder and we hadn't a hope in hell of saving the game. We were the last pair and I decided I was going to give my wicket to the deserving and highly talented Don Shepherd rather than anyone else. I took a big swing, the ball

100

hit my box and I was off like a shot when the ball carried to slip. I wonder if many of today's players would do that? And I wasn't special, simply typical of that breed of county cricketers.

It's disgraceful that so much extra and unnecessary pressure is being put on our umpires by people who won't walk. It's time the captains cracked the whip and helped the umpires out. After all, they can only give what they see. It's time we all started putting our own house in order, rather than waiting to have the administrators take us in hand. Our union, the Cricketers' Association, is a very responsible body, run by sensible men like Jack Bannister and John Arlott, and I think we should start thrashing out a code of conduct. Perhaps suspensions might be the answer, though it'll be a sad day when that happens. But it worries me that things which have long been in vogue abroad are happening over here now. I'm a bridge between an era when the game was more enjoyable to play and the modern version, so I can appreciate the gulf more than most – and it's not just nostalgia at work, because I'm not a sentimental person. Perhaps it's up to an elder statesman like me to get up off my backside at the Association's AGM next spring and tell my 200-odd colleagues that we should start sorting ourselves out.

Of course money has complicated the situation, as well as the influx of overseas players who are used to poor umpiring at home and just don't walk on principle. I wonder what would happen if some batsmen were sponsored for each run they scored? They'd never walk, they'd have to be sent off the field!

I don't like to see professional cricketers categorised as bad sports and money-grabbers. I'm very worried about the image of the game and deeply conscious that it's part of our heritage. Without the game of cricket England wouldn't be the same, and we must do something to clean up our image. When you get MCC members assaulting our best umpires at the centenary test, it's time to start worrying about our game. One remark at the end of the season summed up the attraction of county cricket. It was at Brighton when we had our end-of-season party. Jimmy Gould, one of our members who lives down there, came to the party and he brought his girl friend along. She was telling us that it's no longer safe to walk down the streets of Brighton at night in case she got attacked, then she looked over at Bert Avery as he puffed at his fag, took a

101

swill of his pint and listened to yet another cricket yarn. 'You know,' she said, 'when I look at someone like him, I feel completely safe. He represents all that's decent and tolerant about cricket. When I read of the things that are going on in cricket at the moment, I can't believe it.' It's time we all worked a little harder at putting decency and tolerance back into cricket, or we'll lose supporters like that girl.

Other things worried me about the 1980 season. The wickets were the slowest I've known and not enough good young players seem to be coming through. I can only pick out Richard Williams, Colin Wells, Peter Hacker and Nick Cook of the many English youngsters I've played against in 1980. Otherwise it's the same old faces. We need some more Bothams breaking through. The reduction in the number of overseas players allowed to play in county cricket is long overdue. Just once in a while it would be nice to hear a supporter say, 'Those are our lads out there,' not 'Let's take a look at Proctershire or Riceshire.' No offence meant to the many marvellous overseas players I've enjoyed in the English game, but if you accept that an improved standard of performance by England in test cricket is important, then it's about time we helped those English players get the best batting places and the new ball. Now that Mike Procter is officially qualified for England, it does mean we can sign another overseas player, although in that case we would have to drop one of our Pakistanis in 1981 and both of them in 1982. Purely from a personal point of view, I can understand the criticism of opportunism, although as a Gloucestershire player, if it keeps Procter on our staff for a few more years that must be good for us. Not for one minute do I think Proc will ever play for England and in my heart of hearts I do feel that playing for England is for the English unless, like Basil D'Oliveira, you're denied your rightful place in another society and you also have a British passport.

There's been a lot of talk about slow over-rates and I'm not all that sympathetic with the criticism. Take the test matches. I wonder how many really felt cheated by the West Indies' rate of about thirteen overs an hour? After all, the public were watching the greatest fast-bowling combination ever to bowl in England in my opinion. Nobody twists their arms to turn up at the Oval, Lord's etc to see the West Indians, but they come along in droves to see the world champions. In county cricket I

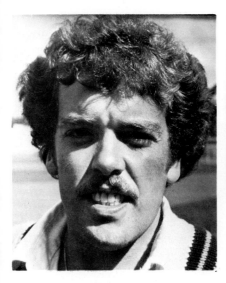

Four of the most promising youngsters I have seen on the county circuit during 1980. Above left, Richard Williams (Northants); above right, Colin Wells (Sussex); below left, Peter Hacker (Nottinghamshire); below right, Nick Cook (Leicestershire).

Some Gloucestershire players and their wives sample the delights of a sponsor's tent after the day's play has ended at Bristol. From the left, Chris Broad, his wife, Carole, Andy Brassington with daughter Emma and wife Ros, Alan Wilkins, his wife, Dot, Phil Bainbridge and his wife, Barbara.

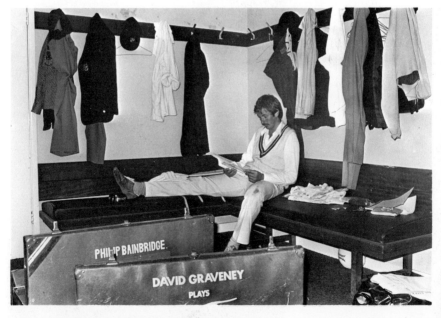

Throughout the summer David Graveney would swot for his accountancy exams, due at the end of the season.

Phil Bainbridge went back as a batsman in the 1980 season but he developed in two ways: as a medium-pace bowler with the ability to bowl fine off-cutters (above), and as a keen amateur photographer (below).

Chris Broad (above) was one of our few plusses among the batsmen in the 1980 season. His off-side play was particularly impressive, as you can judge from scorer Bert Avery's chart of his hundred against Warwickshire in the championship match at Edgbaston (below).

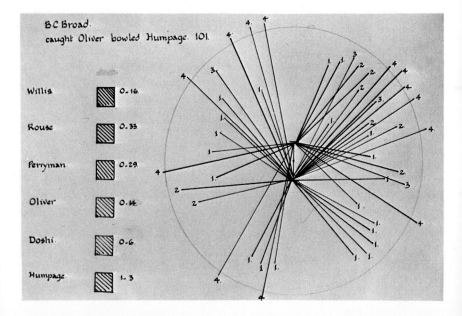

believe that the top three teams in the table should be immune from fines for slow over-rates; after all, they're up there because they've bowled sides out, so why should success be penalised? In modern county cricket most matches are won by seam bowling, so there's pressure on the captain to rush through an extra three or four overs a day instead of giving the seamers a chance to take a breather as they walk back. I suppose I'm biased because I'm a seam bowler, but I think the game should be played properly. It's funny how considerations like over-rates go out the window when the team's winning: Middlesex, Surrey and Sussex, three of the top four sides in the championship, were all fined because they fell under nineteen overs an hour. That's because seam bowlers send down more overs than most in winning county matches.

It's time the county championship was overhauled in favour of a brand of cricket that will benefit the very top of our profession – test cricket. The hundred-over limit on the first innings should be scrapped; it's been in operation since 1974 and it hasn't really benefited our young players, especially with the overseas men grabbing all the prime positions in the batting order and the bowling rota. On a flat wicket the game gets very defensive after a few overs and the bowlers just opt for containment. That's no way to train people to bowl out class batsmen in a five-day test. We should go for sixteen four-day county matches, with the onus for the shape of the match entirely on the shoulders of the captains. The closer our England hopefuls play to five-day cricket, the better for them; they'll have longer to bat and also the incentive to learn the skills and variety needed to dismiss good batsmen. And in the event of a rainy spell, there's also that extra day available, compared to the present three-day structure.

I also believe that the counties should regionalise their seasons, to cut down on travelling and hotel costs. Sometimes we have to travel 250 miles on a Saturday night to play a John Player League game, which may be rained off, and then it's back on Sunday night to pick up the pieces of the county championship match. That's daft. Certain sides should go north for a fortnight and others head south for the same period, while Glamorgan, Somerset and Gloucestershire could provide competition in the west for the same length of time. That's beginning to sort itself out in recent seasons, but anything that

103

can eliminate the worst hassle of all in county cricket – travelling – will be warmly welcomed by the players.

Until the 1980 season I was against the notion of a cricket manager. I thought it a bit of a gimmick and couldn't see what he would do to justify a large salary. But after watching sides like Warwickshire under David Brown and Surrey under Mickey Stewart, I'm convinced they're a good idea. In the modern game there's only so much a captain can do, even with the coach's assistance. Often an experienced manager can spot things on the field that have passed by the skipper's attention, and a few words at the interval can be invaluable provided the captain and manager enjoy a close relationship. It's worked wonders at Edgbaston, where Warwickshire were a revelation in the limited-over matches because they played to a clearly defined plan worked out by Brown and Willis.

At this time of the year it's always sad to see some well-loved blokes go from the county scene. It's even sadder this season because three of my favourite umpires are also retiring. The rules say that John Langridge, Lloyd Budd and Tom Spencer are too old and must stand down – but they're better than some umpires still on the list. I suppose it's a fact of life that if you're too old you must fade away, but it does seem a shame that they're leaving the game when they've got so much still to offer. I'll always remember Lloyd Budd for his encouragement of bowlers, especially if they were having a bad time. Pat Pocock is trying to get him reinstated and I hope he succeeds because Lloyd was the epitome of honesty. So was Tom Spencer, a less gentle character than Lloyd but always very good value. John Langridge has been associated with county cricket since he joined Sussex in 1928; he's already retired once but they couldn't get a better man, so they reinstated him. I wonder if that will happen again for these three great umpires?

Some good players have also retired: Geoff Cope, Mike Taylor, Arnold Long, Tony Cordle, Bob Stephenson and Mike Denness. Jim Watts says he's retiring but I'll believe that when I see it – he'll be making a comeback at fifty! I'm particularly sorry to see my old team-mate, Van Holder, depart the county scene. He was a very fine seamer with Worcestershire and the West Indies; he had pace, ability, accuracy and he taught me a lot. In fact, I've been a lucky man to open the bowling with men like Procter, Holder, Flavell and Coldwell. I must still be adequate at my job, otherwise Gloucestershire wouldn't have just offered me another two-year contract. I signed with pleasure, enthusiasm and the hope that when I do leave the game, I won't have to be carried out. Of the regular county players left in the game, only Norman Gifford, Ken Higgs and Alan Jones are older than me. I wonder which of us will last longest? Perhaps I might get down to some winter training one of these years. But isn't that where we came in?

Statistical Appendix:
Gloucestershire C.C.C., 1980

Schweppes County Championship

	P.	W.	L.	D.	Bt.	Bl.	Pts.
Middlesex (13)	22	10	2	10	58	80	285
Surrey (3)	22	10	4	8	51	74	245
Notts (9)	22	6	5	11	42	64	178
Sussex (4)	22	4	3	15	60	60	168
Somerset (8)	22	3	5	14	56	70	168
Yorkshire (7)	22	4	3	15	51	64	163
Gloucestershire (10)	*22*	*4*	*5*	*13*	*39*	*74*	*161*
Essex (1)	22	4	3	15	48	64	160
Derbyshire (16)	22	4	3	15	47	62	157
Leicestershire (6)	22	4	2	16	45	58	157
Worcestershire (2)	22	3	7	12	54	61	151
Northamptonshire (11)	22	5	4	13	41	47	148
Glamorgan (17)	22	4	4	14	43	57	148
Warwickshire (15)	22	3	4	15	55	54	145
Lancashire (13)	22	4	3	25	26	58	132
Kent (5)	22	2	8	12	36	59	119
Hampshire (12)	22	1	10	11	34	56	102

(1979 positions in brackets)

April 30, May 1, 2, at Worcester. Gloucestershire 250 for 6 dec. (Broad 62) and 62 for 0; Worcestershire 361 for 5 dec. (Turner 228*, Hemsley 61). Match drawn.

May 3, 5, 6, at Bristol. Gloucestershire 287 (Zaheer 104, A. Stovold 89) and 228 for 4 dec. (Procter 88*, Sadiq 61, A. Stovold 51); Northants 208 (Yardley 51, Graveney 5 for 74) and 310 for 2 (Lamb 113*, Williams 80*). Northants won by 8 wkts.

May 7, 8, 9, at Bristol. Gloucestershire 180 (Sadiq 56, Nash 5 for 58) and 220 (Zaheer 93, Nash 6 for 72); Glamorgan 125 (Brain 6 for 68) and 276 for 3 (Miandad 141, Featherstone 73*). Glamorgan won by 7 wkts.

May 24, 26, 27, at Taunton. Somerset 534 for 6 (Botham 228, Denning 98, Gavaskar 75, Taylor 57*); Gloucestershire 239 (Hignell 80, Zaheer 62) and 394 for 5 (Zaheer 173, Hignell 100*, Sadiq 55). Match drawn.

May 28, 29, 30, at Leicester. Leicestershire 206 (Clift 51, Brain 5 for 70) and 224 for 4 dec. (Tolchard 61*, Briers 54); Gloucestershire 179 (Steele 7 for 29) and 91 for 7. Match drawn.

May 31, June 2, 3, at Gloucester. Gloucestershire 220 for 9 dec. (A. Stovold 60) and 88 for 2 (Sadiq 55*); Essex 335 for 9 dec. (Gooch 134, Denness 87, Childs 6 for 90). Match drawn.

June 7, 9, 10, at Northampton. Gloucestershire 342 for 7 dec. (Hignell 89, Zaheer 79, Bainbridge 71, Sarfraz 5 for 65) and 182 (Zaheer 75, Williams 6 for 65); Northants 302 for 7 dec. (Yardley 100*) and 225 for 4 (Larkins 127). Northants won by 6 wkts.

June 14, 16, 17, at Bristol. Gloucestershire v Derbyshire. Abandoned without a ball bowled.

June 18, 19, 20, at Bristol. Gloucestershire 155 and 200 (Malone 5 for 57); Lancashire 143 and 126 for 3 (Kennedy 73*). Match drawn.

June 21, 23, 24, at Bournemouth. Gloucestershire 175; Hampshire 132 for 7. Match drawn.

June 28, 30, July 1, at Guildford. Gloucestershire 157 (Jackman 5 for 41); Surrey 80 for 3. Match drawn.

July 5, 7, 8, at Bristol. Nottinghamshire 275 (Rice 74, Randall 58, Hassan 50) and 138 for 6 dec; Gloucestershire 144 (Zaheer 55, Hacker 5 for 46) and 89 for 8. Match drawn.

July 12, 14, 15, at Bristol. Gloucestershire 101 and 234 (Procter 75); Sussex 167 (Greig 50*, Procter 5 for 81) and 172 for 8 (Graveney 6 for 71). Sussex won by 2 wkts.

July 26, 28, 29, at Sheffield. Yorkshire 153 for 8 dec. and 243 for 1 dec. (Athey 125*, Lumb 101); Gloucestershire 201 for 4 dec. (Broad 79, Sadiq 66). Match drawn.

August 2, 4, 5, at Cheltenham. Gloucestershire 305 (Broad 116, Sadiq 52) and 175 for 3 dec. (Sadiq 90*); Hampshire 178 (Wilkins 5 for 50) and 103 (Graveney 5 for 24). Gloucestershire won by 197 runs.

August 6, 7, 8, at Cheltenham. Gloucestershire 178 (Procter 73, Inchmore 5 for 62) and 177; Worcestershire 111 (Turner 57, Procter 7 for 16) and 148 (Ormrod 53, Procter 7 for 60). Gloucestershire won by 96 runs.

August 9, 11, 12, at Cheltenham. Middlesex 220 (Brain 5 for 46) and 158 for 4 dec. (Brearley 54); Gloucestershire 109 (Daniel 5 for 32) and 271 for 4 (Procter 134*). Gloucestershire won by 6 wkts.

August 16, 18, 19, at Swansea. Gloucestershire 146 and 236 (Procter 88, Zaheer 50, Nash 7 for 79); Glamorgan 212 (Featherstone 107) and 171 for 2 (Hopkins 64*). Glamorgan won by 8 wkts.

August 20, 21, 22, at Folkestone. Gloucestershire 206 (Johnson 5 for 70) and 159 (Zaheer 98, Johnson 5 for 41); Kent 162 (Childs 5 for 61) and 148. Gloucestershire won by 55 runs.

August 23, 25, 26, at Bristol. Gloucestershire 309 (Procter 57, Graveney 55, Dredge 5 for 95) and 317 (Sadiq 92, Procter 84, A. Stovold 80, Marks 5 for 77); Somerset 426 (Richards 170, Roebuck 101) and 200 for 7 (Lloyds 64). Match drawn.

August 27, 28, 29, at Edgbaston. Gloucestershire 311 for 9 (Broad 101, A. Stovold 59, Procter 52) and 143 for 4 (Sadiq 59*); Warwickshire 182 (Smith 56). Match drawn.

September 3, 4, 5, at Hove. Sussex 353 (Barclay 115, Wells 65, Wilkins 5 for 76) and 147 for 1 (Mendis 81*, Wessels 53*); Gloucestershire 250 for 6 dec. (A. Stovold 85, Broad 65). Match drawn.

Other first-class matches

April 23, 24, 25, at Oxford. Gloucestershire 319 for 3 dec. (Broad 120, M. Stovold 75*, Hignell 63*) and 260 for 4 dec. (Graveney 119); Oxford University 79 and 158 (Orders 70*, Graveney 6 for 49). Gloucestershire won by 342 runs.

July 2, 3, 4, at Bristol. West Indies 278 (Garner 104, D. L. Murray 64) and 169 (Bacchus 69); Gloucestershire 183 (Sadiq 76, Graveney 50) and 198. West Indies won by 58 runs.

First-class averages

Batting

	M.	I.	N.O.	R.	H.S.	Ave.	Catches
B. M. Brain	22	26	5	185	37	8.81	3
A. J. Brassington	23	30	8	113	14	5.14	45
P. Bainbridge	17	29	2	472	71	15.63	12
B. C. Broad	20	35	1	961	120	28.26	7
J. H. Childs	15	19	10	44	8	4.89	6
D. A. Graveney	21	31	7	513	119	21.38	8
A. J. Hignell	15	23	5	630	100	35.00	11
M. D. Partridge	11	18	6	286	48	23.83	4
M. J. Procter	19	33	2	1081	134	34.87	17
Sadiq Mohammad	22	40	4	1172	92	32.56	27
A. W. Stovold	22	39	2	958	89	25.89	10
M. W. Stovold	5	8	2	137	75	22.83	0
D. Surridge	1			did not bat			0
A. H. Wilkins	19	24	3	262	44	12.48	8
S. J. Windaybank	1	2	0	63	43	31.50	1
Zaheer Abbas	20	35	1	1296	173	38.12	4

Bowling

	O.	M.	R.	W.	Ave.
Brain	525.5	104	1609	57	28.23
Bainbridge	144.4	22	504	15	33.60
Broad	28.0	8	109	3	36.33
Childs	373.4	98	1034	43	24.05
Graveney	554.4	152	1598	55	29.06
Hignell	9.0	1	29	1	29.00
Partridge	161.5	36	572	11	52.00
Procter	372.1	102	931	51	18.25

	O.	M.	R.	W.	Ave.
Sadiq	54.5	3	252	1	252.00
A.Stovold	4.4	0	24	0	——
Surridge	21.0	11	33	4	8.25
Wilkins	393.5	86	1245	52	23.94
Zaheer	11.0	3	46	2	23.00

Gillette Cup

First round. A bye.

Second round. July 16, at the Oval. Surrey 200 (Knight 59); Gloucestershire 192 for 9 (Procter 52). Surrey won by 8 runs.

John Player League

	P.	W.	L.	N.R.	T.	Pts.
Warwickshire (17)	16	11	4	0	1	46
Somerset (1)	16	11	5	0	0	44
Middlesex (4)	16	10	5	1	0	42
Leicestershire (6)	16	9	6	1	0	38
Surrey (12)	16	8	6	2	0	36
Derbyshire (16)	16	8	7	1	0	34
Northamptonshire (12)	16	8	7	1	0	34
Worcestershire (3)	16	8	7	1	0	34
Sussex (12)	16	6	6	4	0	32
Gloucestershire (8)	*16*	*7*	*8*	*1*	*0*	*30*
Hampshire (10)	16	6	8	2	0	28
Kent (2)	16	6	8	1	1	28
Lancashire (10)	16	6	9	1	0	26
Essex (6)	16	6	10	0	0	24
Nottinghamshire (8)	16	6	10	0	0	24
Yorkshire (4)	16	6	10	0	0	24
Glamorgan (12)	16	4	10	2	0	20

(1979 positions in brackets)

May 4, at Bristol. Northants 186 for 5 (Williams 51); Gloucestershire 172 for 9. Northants won by 14 runs.

May 18, at Leicester. Leicestershire 204 for 8; Gloucestershire 126. Leicestershire won by 78 runs.

May 25, at Old Trafford. Gloucestershire 166 for 6; Lancashire 170 for 2 (Lloyd 90*, Hayes 67*). Lancashire won by 8 wkts.

June 1, at Gloucester. Gloucestershire 150 for 8 (Sadiq 54, Procter 51); Essex 118. Gloucestershire won by 32 runs.

June 8, at Canterbury. Gloucestershire 140 for 8 (Zaheer 68); Kent 141 for 5 (Cowdrey 52). Kent won by 5 wkts.

June 15, at Bristol. Gloucestershire 213 for 3 (Zaheer 112*, Procter 58); Worcestershire 211 (Neale 84). Gloucestershire won by 2 runs.

June 29, at Guildford. Gloucestershire 133; Surrey 92. Gloucestershire won by 41 runs.

July 6, at Bristol. Nottinghamshire 188 for 3 (Rice 60*); Gloucestershire 171 for 5 (Zaheer 79). Gloucestershire won by 5 wkts. on a reduced target.

July 13, at Moreton-in-Marsh. Gloucestershire 200 for 8 (Procter 79); Sussex did not bat. Match abandoned.

July 20, at Edgbaston. Warwickshire 150 for 8; Gloucestershire 149 for 6. Warwickshire won by 1 run.

July 27, at Hull. Gloucestershire 232 for 4 (Zaheer 104*, Procter 61); Yorkshire 233 for 4 (Ingram 87*). Yorkshire won by 6 wkts.

August 3, at Cheltenham. Hampshire 182 for 8 (Rice 63); Gloucestershire 173 for 8. Gloucestershire won by 2 wkts. on a reduced target.

August 10, at Cheltenham. Gloucestershire 183 for 8 (Zaheer 81*); Middlesex 128. Gloucestershire won by 55 runs.

August 17, at Swansea. Gloucestershire 184 for 7 (Zaheer 103); Glamorgan 122 for 8. Gloucestershire won on faster scoring rate.

August 24, at Bristol. Gloucestershire 179 for 8 (Procter 57, Broad 54); Somerset 183 for 9. Somerset won by 1 wkt.

September 7, at Chesterfield. Gloucestershire 154 for 6 (A. Stovold 62*); Derbyshire 155 for 4 (Miller 76*). Derbyshire won by 6 wkts.

Benson and Hedges Cup

May 10, at Bristol. Glamorgan 228 for 8; Gloucestershire 227 for 8 (Procter 50). Glamorgan won by 1 run.

May 14, at Hove. Sussex 238 for 5 (Mendis 109, Imran 55); Gloucestershire 229 for 7 (A. Stovold 61*, Zaheer 60). Sussex won by 9 runs.

May 17, at Bristol. Essex 224 (Gooch 62, Hardie 53); Gloucestershire 225 for 5 (A. Stovold 73*). Gloucestershire won by 5 wkts.

May 22, at Chippenham. Minor Counties 212 for 8 (Cairns 54); Gloucestershire 209. Minor Counties won by 3 runs.

Index

111

Guyana 92

Hacker, Peter 51, 52, 102, 107
Hadlee, Richard 52, 53
Halesowen 44
Hampshire C.C.C. 14, 45–6, 61, 63, 95, 106, 107, 109
Hanley Castle 21
Harris, Mike 52, 53
hat tricks 50, 56
Hayes, F. 29
Haynes, Desmond 39, 91
Headley, R. G. A. 100
Healey, Denis 99
Hemmings, Eddie 51, 52
Hemsley, E. J. O. 69
Henderson 68
Hendrick, M. 8, 39, 81, 82
Higgs, Ken 34, 105
Hignell, A. J.: averages 108; batting qualities 30–1, 41, 61, 106; Cambridge graduate 14; candidate for captaincy 64; pastimes 36; other references 10, 12, 17, 48, 97
Hobbs, Robin 91
Hogg, Willie 29–30
Holder, Vanburn viii, 100, 104
Holding, Michael 40, 50, 90
Holts Products 49
Honolulu 90
horse-racing 17, 33
Horton, M. J. 100
Hove 23, 94
Hull 63
Humpage, G. W. 58
Humphries, D. ('Humpty') 14, 42, 43, 68

Ilkeston 54
Illingworth, Ray 60, 93
Imran Khan Niazi 24, 62, 88
Inchmore, John 42, 43

Jackman, Robin 30, 45, 56, 96
Jackson, Les 100
Jamaica 92
Javed Miandad Khan 19, 21, 24, 41, 74, 106
Jesty, Trevor 46
John Player League 18, 22, 34, 36, 41, 47, 48, 51, 55, 56, 57, 61, 66, 72, 74, 84, 89, 96, 97, 109
Jones, Alan 20, 21, 74–5, 105
Jones, Barry 14
journalists, cricket 8, 10, 23, 50–1, 79–80

Kallicharran, Alvin 49–50, 58
Kennington Oval 90, 92, *see also* Oval, The
Kent C.C.C. 6, 39, 47, 75–7, 95, 106, 107, 109
Kenyon, D. 100
Kirsten, Peter 89
Knight, Roger 8, 46, 56, 68, 69, 109
Knott, Alan 40, 76, 77, 81, 97

Lamb, Allan 15–17, 41
Lamb, Tim 17, 59
Lancashire C.C.C. 29, 36, 44, 61, 95, 106, 109
Langridge, John 104
Larkins, Wayne 15, 107
Lee, Peter 29
left-handed batsmen 68
Leicestershire C.C.C. 25, 61, 84, 106, 109
le Roux, Garth 24, 55, 62
Lewis, Richard 6
Lillee, D. 7, 8, 36, 62
limited-over matches 3, 9, 11, 28, 30, 46, 56, 57, 60, 88, 92
Lister, Joe 27
Lloyd, A. 50, 58
Lloyd, D. 30
Long, Arnold 104
Lord's 11, 24, 41, 52, 79, 88
Lumb, Richard 8, 59

Malawi 62, 90
Malone, Mick 44
managers 26, 29, 104
Marks, Vic 7, 30, 107
Marsh, Rodney 85
Marshall, M. D. 46
Marylebone Cricket Club 101
May, P. 7, 14, 81, 100
Mead, Lex 75, 79
Melford, Michael 8
Mendis, G. D. 23, 24, 88, 108, 110
Meyer, Barry 13, 14
Middlesex C.C.C. 41, 48, 52, 69, 73, 96, 103, 106, 107, 109
Miller, Geoff 30, 89, 93, 110
Minor Counties XI 7, 27, 31, 34, 110
Moreton-in-Marsh 43, 55
Moseley, Ezra 74
Moseley, Hallam 79
Moss, Alan 100
Mushtaq Mohammad 59

Nash, Malcolm 19, 74

113